August Wilson

SAMUEL FRENCH, INC.

45 WEST 25TH STREET   NEW YORK 10010

7623 SUNSET BOULEVARD HOLLYWOOD 90046

LONDON   TORONTO

IMPORTANT BILLING AND CREDIT REQUIREMENTS

Originally Produced on Broadway
by

SAGEWORKS

Benjamin Mordecai, Executive Director
Center Theatre Group/Ahmanson Theatre,
Gordon Davidson, Artistic Director
Herb Alpert/Margo Lion   Scott Rudin/Paramount Pictures
and Jujamcyn Theatres
in association with
Goodman Theatre, Huntington Theatre Company,
American Conservatory Theatre and Manhattan Theatre Club

● ● ● ● ● ● ● ● ● ● ● ● ● ● ● ● ● ●

⚅ WALTER KERR THEATRE

A JUJAMCYN THEATRE

JAMES H. BINGER
CHAIRMAN

ROCCO LANDESMAN
PRESIDENT

PAUL LIBIN
PRODUCING DIRECTOR

JACK VIERTEL
CREATIVE DIRECTOR

SAGEWORKS
Benjamin Mordecai, Executive Producer

Center Theatre Group / Ahmanson Theatre, Gordon Davidson, Artistic Director
Herb Alpert / Margo Lion   Scott Rudin / Paramount Pictures
and Jujamcyn Theatres

in association with
Goodman Theatre, Huntington Theatre Company,
American Conservatory Theatre and Manhattan Theatre Club

present

KEITH DAVID

in

August Wilson's

SEVEN GUITARS

with

ROSALYN
COLEMAN

VIOLA
DAVIS

TOMMY
HOLLIS

ROGER
ROBINSON

MICHELE
SHAY

and

RUBEN SANTIAGO-HUDSON

set design by
SCOTT BRADLEY

costume design by
CONSTANZA ROMERO

lighting design by
CHRISTOPHER AKERLIND

musical direction by
DWIGHT ANDREWS

sound design by
TOM CLARK

production stage manager
JANE E. NEUFELD

casting by
MEG SIMON

technical supervision
GENE O'DONOVAN

press representative
**BONEAU/
BRYAN-BROWN**

general management
MARSHALL B. PURDY

directed by

LLOYD RICHARDS

AUGUST WILSON'S SEVEN GUITARS was originally presented at the
National Playwright's Conference of the Eugene O'Neill Theatre Center

CAST OF CHARACTERS

CANEWELL
RED CARTER
VERA DOTSON
LOUISE
HEDLEY
FLOYD "SCHOOLBOY" BARTON
RUBY

THE SETTING:

The action of the play takes place in the backyard of a house in Pittsburgh in 1948. It is a brick house with a single window fronting the yard. Access to the room is gained by stairs leading to a small porch on the side of the house. This is VERA'S apartment. LOUISE and HEDLEY live on the second floor in separate quarters which are accessed by steps leading to a landing and a flight of stairs alongside the building. The stairs are wooden and are in need of repair. The yard is closely flanked on both sides by the neighboring buildings. A ten-foot high fence stage right blocks our view into the yard at stage right and a four-foot high fence is at stage left. The yard is a dirt yard with a small garden area marked off by bricks in the downstage right corner where VERA has made a garden of vegetables and flowers. A cellar door leads into the basement where HEDLEY stores his gear. Off to the side and in the back of the yard is a contraption made of bricks, wood and corrugated sheet metal, which is where HEDLEY kills chickens. It doubles as a grill for cooking and when it is not being used, it breaks down with a minimum of parts left standing. During several of his scenes HEDLEY builds or dismantles his contraption and stores its pieces in the cellar. There is an entrance to the yard through a latched gate to the left of the building. There is occasionally a card table set up in the yard with an eclectic mix of chairs. Several light bulbs, rigged by way of extension cords, run from VERA'S apartment to light the table so they can sit and play cards on the hot summer nights of 1948.

ACT I

Scene 1

(The lights come up on CANEWELL, VERA, LOUISE, RED CARTER, and HEDLEY gathered in the yard, dressed in their Sunday best. They have come from the cemetery where they buried FLOYD BARTON. There is lingering evidence of food and drink. A rare moment of silence has settled on the yard. LOUISE, in a much needed affirmation of life, begins singing a bawdy song.)

LOUISE. *(Sings.)*
"Anybody here wanna try my cabbage
just step this way
Anybody here like to try my cabbage
just holler Hey."
RED CARTER. Hey!
LOUISE. *(Sings.)*
"I gave some to the parson
and he shook with glee
He took a collection
and gave it all to me
Anybody here wanna try good cabbage
just step this way."

7

(A sweet potato pie sits on the table RED CARTER takes a piece.)

CANEWELL. Uh Huh, put that back Red! That's my piece!

RED CARTER. How's this yours when I got it.

CANEWELL. I had my eye on that piece.

RED CARTER. You had your eye on it and I had my hand on it. That go to show you the hand is quicker than the eye.

VERA. There's plenty to go around. Here, Canewell.

(VERA hands CANEWELL a piece of pie.)

RED CARTER. I sure was hungry.

CANEWELL. I didn't eat nothing this morning.

LOUISE. It was hard to eat. I ain't felt like eating nothing either. But I said, "Let me go on and eat something cause I don't know how long it be before I eat again."

CANEWELL. I want Reverend Thompson to preach my funeral. He make everything sound pretty.

RED CARTER. I was just thinking the same thing! He almost make it where you want to die just to have somebody talk over you like that.

CANEWELL. It sound like he reading from the bible even when he ain't. I told myself Floyd would have liked that if he could have heard it.

VERA. Did you see them angels out there at the cemetery?

RED CARTER. Uh oh, Vera done saw some angels.

CANEWELL. I saw them out there too. They look like they was with the funeral home only they wasn't. Wasn't that them Vera? Had on black hats.

VERA. They come down out the sky.

CANEWELL. I seen them. I know who you talking about. One of them come and ask me how to get to Floyd's house.

RED CARTER. Somebody ask me the same thing. One of them men at the funeral.

CANEWELL. Did he have a black hat? Look like he was with the funeral home. Had kinda bushy eyebrows?

RED CARTER. Yeah. Had on a black tie.

CANEWELL. That's him. What did you tell him?

RED CARTER. I told him the truth. I didn't know where Floyd was staying at. He was staying in Chicago. Sometime he was staying here. Then he was staying over there. Next time he be staying around the corner somewhere.

CANEWELL. I told him I didn't see where it mattered too much seeing as how he wasn't home. He just kinda looked at me funny. I believe that's when he went over and started talking to you.

LOUISE. I ain't seen no angels. You all ain't seen none either. Red, did you see any angels out there?

VERA. There was six of them. They come down out the sky.

CANEWELL. They did just kind of show up. Like you looked around and they was standing there. Trying to act like they had been there all the time.

LOUISE. Hey, Hedley, Vera seen some angels at the cemetery.

CANEWELL. Hey, Vera... they was all dressed alike? Look like they might have been brothers?

RED CARTER. Maybe they was some of Foster's brothers. If they was with the funeral home.

HEDLEY. I seen them too.

CANEWELL. Hedley seen them. Louise... you didn't see

them men in black suits always fussing about everything?

LOUISE. They was with the funeral home, fool!

CANEWELL. Naw,... they wasn't with the funeral home. They *seem* like they was with the funeral home. I don't know who they was. If they was with the funeral home I would have seen them before. They just kinda showed up. Just like you turn around and they was there.

VERA. They carried Floyd away. I seen them.

CANEWELL. When it come time to throw the dirt in the grave seem like they didn't want nobody to do it but them? They tried to crowd everybody out. I say to myself, "It don't seem right not to throw some dirt in the grave." I figure it was better if I throw it in than if some stranger throw it in. They didn't say anything. I just pushed on past them, scooped up a handful of dirt and threw it down in the grave. I could hear it when it hit the casket. It was kinda wet and it made a sound when it hit. I say, "You was a good old boy... but you dead and gone."

VERA. They carried Floyd right on up in the sky.

RED CARTER. That go to show you I don't know too much about nothing. Cause I always swore Floyd was going straight to hell.

CANEWELL. You know... I ask myself... I wonder did he know?

VERA. The bible say some things ain't for you to know. It say you know neither the day nor the hour when death come.

CANEWELL. He come like a thief in the night. And he don't go away empty. There's a song what go—*(CANEWELL sings.)*

He'll come to your house
he won't stay long

You look in the bed
find your mother gone
CANEWELL. *(cont.)* Your mother. Sister. Brother. Friend.
I don't believe he knew but then again I do.

RED CARTER, I believe everyman knows something but
most times they don't pay attention to it.

VERA. I believe he knew something too.

LOUISE. Whether he did or not ain't done him no good. It
ain't made no difference one way or the other. It didn't kill him
but then it ain't kept him here either.

RED CARTER. Hey, Vera, give me a beer.

VERA. I ain't got no beer.

(VERA starts into the house.)

CANEWELL. Here, get you a taste of this bourbon. Vera
you going into the house, put on Floyd's record.

RED CARTER. You can get a whole case of beer for two
dollars and fifty cents.

CANEWELL. I know. You can get any kind you want. Iron
City. Duquesne. Black Label. Red Label. Yellow Label. You
can get any kind of label you want. Some kinds do cost a little
more.

RED CARTER. I would have got a case and carried it up
here if I knew Vera didn't have any.

CANEWELL. I should have carried two. One on each
shoulder. If I didn't have this bourbon. I looked at that bourbon and forgot all about that beer.

*(The sound of FLOYD BARTON singing "That's All Right"
comes out of the kitchen window and envelopes the yard.*

There is a moment of silent reverie.)

RED CARTER. Floyd "Schoolboy" Barton.

(The lights fade. The music carries into the next scene.)

Scene 2

*(The lights come up on FLOYD BARTON and VERA DATSUN
dancing in the yard. FLOYD is a young man of thirty-five.
He is a blues singer. VERA is eight years younger than
FLOYD. It is early evening. They are dancing to FLOYD'S
record "That's All Right" which is playing on the radio inside the house. A rooster is heard crowing intermittently
throughout the scene.)*

FLOYD. *(Singing on the radio.)*
"You told me baby once upon a time
you said if I would be yours
you would sure be mine
but that's alright..."
FLOYD. Listen... hear that?
VERA. It sound just like you.
FLOYD. Comeon, now... you supposed to lean back.

(FLOYD bends VERA back pushing his pelvis into hers.)

VERA. Comeon, Floyd!

FLOYD. *(Singing.)*
"You told me baby once upon a time
you said if I would be yours
you would sure be mine
but that's alright..."
This the way you supposed to dance to my record. You supposed to act like you know something about it.

(VERA tries to break away. FLOYD hold her closer.)

FLOYD. *(Singing.)*
"But that's alright
I know you in love with another man
but that's alright..."

(FLOYD tries to kiss her.)

VERA. Floyd, stop it now. Don't be doing all that.

(VERA breaks away.)

FLOYD. Come here. *(He pulls her to him.)* I'll never jump back on you in life.

VERA. I don't want to hear it.

FLOYD. I just say I'll never jump back on you. If you give me a chance I'll prove it to you.

VERA. You done had more than enough chances.

FLOYD. Did you get that letter I sent you?

VERA. What you doing writing me a letter?

FLOYD. I knew that would surprise you. I say, "Vera gonna be surprised to see my name on the envelope." I sure wish I could have seen your face.

VERA. Had somebody writing all them lies.

FLOYD. Didn't it sound good? I like the way that sound. It cost me fifty cents. Some fellow down the workhouse be writing everybody letters. He read it back to me. I say, "Vera ain't never heard me say nothing like this." That be the kind of stuff I want to say but can't think to say. It sounded so good I started to give him an extra quarter. I say I'm gonna wait and see what Vera say.

VERA. He ought to have gave you your money back if it depend on what Vera say. I done told you my feet ain't on backwards.

FLOYD. My feet ain't on backwards either. I just got to missing you so bad. My life got so empty without you.

VERA. Floyd, I don't want to hear that. Just stop it right now.

FLOYD. What? Stop what? I'm telling the truth.

VERA. Go tell it to Pearl Brown.

FLOYD. See, you wanna bring all that up. I told you about all that in the letter. Pearl Brown don't mean nothing to me.

VERA. She sure meant something to you before. She meant enough to you for you to pack up your clothes and drag her to Chicago with you. She meant something to you then. Talking about you gonna send for me when you got up there. Left out of here telling me them lies and had her waiting around the corner.

FLOYD. She wasn't waiting around the corner.

VERA. She may as well have been. She might be waiting around there now for all I know.

FLOYD. Comeon now, Vera. You know better than that.

VERA. If you going back to Chicago... then just go ahead.

FLOYD. I got to go back. The record company up there waiting on me. They done sent me a letter telling me to come on back. I wanna go back and take you with me. I ain't gonna be here long. I just got to get my guitar out the pawnshop. I might have to pawn my thirty-eight. You still got my thirty-eight don't you?

VERA. It's in there where you put it. I ain't touched it.

FLOYD. I sat down there doing them ninety days, I told myself it's a good thing I didn't have that with me when they arrested me. Talking about vagrancy... if I had that thirty-eight they would have tried to dig a hole and put me under the jail. As it was they took me down there and charged me with worthlessness. Canewell had five dollars in his pocket and they let him go. Took me down there and give me ninety days.

VERA. Canewell say you threatened to burn down the jail house. That's why they give you ninety days.

FLOYD. They got that all mixed up. I asked one of the guards to show me the back door in case there was a fire. He said the jailhouse don't burn. I told him give me a gallon of gasoline and I'd prove him wrong. He told the judge I threatened to burn down the jailhouse. The judge ain't even asked me about it. He give me ninety days for worthlessness. Say Rockefeller worth a million dollars and you ain't worth two cents. Ninety days in the workhouse. *(FLOYD takes a letter from his pocket.)* Look here... look here. Look what they sent to my sister's house. *(He holds up the letter, bragging.)* It say, "Come on back to Chicago and make some more records." Say... "We'll talk about the details when you get here." *(VERA reaches for the letter.)* Naw... naw. All you got to know is it say come on back. You ain't got to know all my business. *(He shows VERA the envelope.)* Look at that. "Mr. Floyd Barton." You get you a hit record and the white folks call you Mister. Mister Floyd Barton. *(He hands VERA the letter.)* Go on read it. Read it out loud. "Dear Mr. Barton. Our records show... " Go on... read it.

VERA. *(Reading.)*

Dear Mr. Barton:

Our records show you recorded some material for us in August of 1947. We are uncertain of your status. If you are the same Floyd Barton who recorded "That's All Right" and are still in the business we would like to provide another opportunity for you to record. Stop by when you are in Chicago and we can discuss further arrangements. We are Savoy records...

FLOYD. 1115 Federal Avenue in Chicago Illinois.

Sincerely, Wilber H. Gardner, President.

(VERA hands him back the letter.)

VERA. That's nice, Floyd.

FLOYD. I can't go without you.

VERA. I ain't going to no Chicago. You know better than to ask me that. What I want to go up there for?

FLOYD. Wait till you see it. There ain't nothing like it. They got more people than you ever seen. You can't even imagine that many people. Seem like everybody in the world in Chicago. That's only place for a black man to be. That's where I seen Muddy Waters. I was walking past this club and I heard this music. People was pushing and crowding in the club; seem like the place was busting at the seams. I asked somebody, I say, "Who's that?" They told me, "That's Muddy Waters." I took off my hat. I didn't know you could make the music sound like that. That told me say, "The sky's the limit." I told myself say,

"I'm gonna play like that one day." I stayed there until they put me out. Mr. T.L. Hall asked me what I wanted to do. I told him I wanted to play at the Hurricane Club. He say he'd fix it.

VERA. I wouldn't put too much faith in whatever Mr. T.L. Hall say. I ain't never known him to do nothing for you. Call himself your manager. What he ever manage?

FLOYD. That's cause I didn't have a hit record. Its' different now. You get a hit record and you be surprised how everything change. Mr. T.L. Hall done got in touch with Savoy Records to set up a recording date for Chicago. They waiting on me now. Come here.

(FLOYD slides his arm around VERA, she slides away.)

VERA. I told you don't start that.
FLOYD. I want to make you happy. I got something for you.
VERA. It ain't nothing I need.

(VERA breaks off.)

FLOYD. The first time I ever seen you. I never will forget that. You remember that?

VERA. Yeah I remember.

FLOYD. You was looking so pretty.

VERA. Floyd, don't start that. Ain't no need in you going back through that.

FLOYD. Naw, I was just saying... I seen you that first time. You had on that blue dress. I believe it was pink and blue.

VERA. It was two different kinds of blue.

FLOYD. I had just got out the army. They give me forty-seven dollars. Adjustment allowance or something like that. I come up Logan Street and I seen you. That's why I always say I had a pocket full of money when I met you. I seen you and said, "There go a woman." Whatever else you might say... a pretty woman... a nice woman, a not so nice woman... whatever else you might say, you got to put that woman part in there. I say, "Floyd, there go a woman." My hands got to itching and seem like I didn't know what to do with them. I put them in my pocket and felt them forty-seven dollars... that thirty-eight under my coat... and I got up my nerve to say something to you. You remember that? Seem like that was a long time ago.

VERA. I had just left my mama's house.

FLOYD. I knew you was just getting started. But what you don't know, I was just getting started too. I was ready. You was just what I was looking for.

VERA. You was looking for anything you could find.

FLOYD. I said, "That's the kind of woman a man kill somebody over." Then I see you turn and walk toward the door. I said, "They just gonna have to kill me." That's when I went after you. I said you was just right for me and if I could get that I never would want nothing else. That's why you ought to try me one more time. If you try me one more time, you never carry no regrets.

VERA. I don't carry no regrets now. I'm gonna leave it like that.

(VERA starts into the house.)

FLOYD. Comeon, Vera...

VERA. I done been there. Floyd, I ain't going back.

FLOYD. I told you what it was. It wasn't nothing to me. Pearl Brown don't mean nothing to me.

VERA. It wasn't nothing to you but it was something to me. To have you just up and walk out like that. What you think happened to me. Did you ever stop to ask yourself, "I wonder how Vera doing? I wonder how she feel?" I lay here every night in an empty bed. In an empty room. Where? Someplace special? Someplace where you had been? The same room you walked out of? The same bed you turned your back on? You give it up and you want it? What kind of sense does that make?

FLOYD. I told you I could see I was wrong.

VERA. You had what you want and I didn't. That makes you special. You one of them special people who is supposed to have everything just the way they want it.

FLOYD. I see where I was wrong. I told you that. It seemed like she believed in me more.

VERA. You supposed to believe in yourself.

FLOYD. A man that believe in himself still need a woman that believe in him. You can't make life happen without a woman.

VERA. I wanted to be that for you. Floyd. I wanted to know where you was bruised at. So I could be a woman for you. So I could touch you there. So I could spread myself all over you and know that I was a woman. That I could give a man only those things a woman has to give. And he could be satisfied. How much woman you think it make you feel to know you can't satisfy a man?

FLOYD. I ain't about being satisfied.

VERA. So he could say, "Yes, Vera a woman." That's what you say but you never believed it. You never showed me all those places where you were a man. You went to Pearl Brown and you showed her. I don't know what she did or didn't do but I looked up and you was back here after I had given you up. After I had walked through an empty house for a year and a half looking for you. After I would lay myself out on that bed and search my body for your fingerprints. "He touched me here. Floyd touched me here and he touched me here and he touched me here and he kissed me here and he gave me here and he took here and he ain't here he ain't here he ain't here quit looking for him cause he ain't here he's there! there! there! there!

FLOYD. Comeon. Vera... don't do this.

VERA. He's there. In Chicago with another woman and all I have is a little bit of nothing, a little bit of touching, a little bit of myself left. It ain't even here no more what you looking for. What you remember. It ain't even here no more.

FLOYD. It's enough for me. It's all I ever wanted. Even if I couldn't see it. That's why I come back. That's why this time I want to take you with me. I told you about all that. I ain't never wanted to hurt you. Whatever you is, that's enough for me. Okay? Now I don't know what else to say. I ain't too good at talking all this out. Come and go to Chicago with me. I need you real bad. That's all I know to say. I ain't never needed nobody like I need you. I don't want no hit record if I can't have a hit record with you. See? That's all I know to say about Pearl Brown... to say about Chicago... to say about Vera Datsun. I don't want it if I can't have you with it.

VERA. Then you don't want it.

(LOUISE enters carrying a bag of groceries. There is immediate tension between her and FLOYD.)

FLOYD. Hey, Louise.

LOUISE. How you doing, Floyd? You look like you done gained some weight.

FLOYD. A little bit.

LOUISE. Least they feed you down there in the workhouse. What are you going to cook, Vera?

VERA. Chicken. Potatoes and green beans. And some cornbread. Floyd likes his cornbread.

FLOYD. I can eat a whole pan of cornbread. I like cornbread. I like my chicken too. I can eat two or three chickens.

LOUISE. I can look at you and see that.

VERA. I'll fix you up a plate when I cook it up.

LOUISE. That be nice. That way I won't have to cook. I got a letter from my niece. She got into trouble down there in Alabama and she coming to stay with me. I'll tell you about it.

VERA. What kind of trouble.

LOUISE. Man trouble. What other kind of trouble a young woman get into? Somebody done killed some other body and somebody family done did this or that or the other. My sister say it's best she got out of there. I'll tell you about it. Floyd, I can't wait to beat you at a game of whist. You still play whist.

FLOYD. I done got better.

LOUISE. I done got better too.

LOUISE exits. FLOYD puts his arm around VERA.)

FLOYD. I done got better at everything I do.

VERA. I don't see how, seeing as how you ain't had no practice.

FLOYD. Watch.

VERA. Ain't gonna be no watching here.

(VERA exits into the house followed by FLOYD as the lights go down and "That's All Right" comes up on the radio.)

Scene 3

(The lights come up on the yard the next morning. HEDLEY enters from the basement carrying a piece of corrugated tin. He begins to work at setting up the stand where he kills chickens. He makes several trips to the basement. LOUISE enters from the porch. The rooster crows intermittently throughout the scene.)

HEDLEY. *(Sings.)*
"I thought I heard Buddy Bolden say
Here go the money, King,
Take it away..."
LOUISE. Hey, Hedley. What kind of cigarettes you got? Give me a pack of Old Gold. *(HEDLEY doesn't respond. He enters the basement and comes out carrying a crate of live chickens.)* Give me some cigarettes. What kind you got?
HEDLEY. Chesterfield.

(HEDLEY enters the basement and carries out another crate of chickens which he stacks on the top of the other.)

LOUISE. I want some Old Gold.
HEDLEY. I told you, woman. Chesterfields.
LOUISE. Why don't you get some Old Gold? You know I smoke Old Gold. Why you wanna be stubborn?

HEDLEY. The people smoke Chesterfield. The people smoke Lucky Strike. The people smoke Pall Mall. The people smoke Camel. Nobody smoke Old Gold. Who you know smoke Old Gold?

LOUISE. I smoke them. There's a whole lot of people smoke Old Gold. Anybody want a good cigarette smoke Old Gold.

HEDLEY. I got Chesterfield.

(HEDLEY exits into the cellar.)

LOUISE. Give me a pack of them. You seen Floyd? They let him out the workhouse. He come back here talking all that stuff. I hope Vera don't let him back in. He ain't up to no good. She be better off with the iceman... as ugly as he is.

(HEDLEY enters carrying a bucket, an apron, a bag of feathers, and various other tools.)

HEDLEY. I don't see nobody.

(HEDLEY takes a small notebook from his pocket and writes in it.)

LOUISE. He in there. After three months he liable to be in there all day.

(HEDLEY takes a pack of cigarettes from a carton he has in his basket and holds it out to her.)

HEDLEY. That's three dollars and forty cents you owe me.

LOUISE. Oh hush up, man. It's liable to be thirty dollars and forty cents before I pay you. *(HEDLEY puts the cigarettes back.)* You ain't said nothing about paying me for all the biscuits I made you. All them plates of collard greens. Them black eye peas. Give me a pack of them cigarettes! *(HEDLEY hands her the cigarettes.)* I got me a little book too. You ain't the only one got a little book. I'm going up there and look in my little book and see how much you owe me.

HEDLEY. George Butler died. I sell many chicken sandwiches tonight. Many chicken sandwiches. Soon I'm gonna be a big man. You watch.

LOUISE. If you don't pay your rent you gonna be sitting out there on the sidewalk. Talking about being a big man. You gonna be a big man without a roof over your head.

HEDLEY. I always pay my rent, woman. You know that.

LOUISE. You ain't paid it this month. You two days late.

HEDLEY. I pay you tomorrow. Hedley sell plenty plenty chicken sandwiches tonight.

LOUISE. You pay me tomorrow. You know how Bella is about her money. I ain't gonna have her getting on me. And you clean up this yard. I don't want all them chicken feathers around here. And don't you be leaving any of them feet around here either. Did you go down there and see the doctor? You need to go back and see the doctor. You sick. I called them and told them you need to go down there and get tested.

HEDLEY. Hedley not sick no more. I go see Miss Sarah Degree. She give me the root tea. I feel just fine.

LOUISE. You need to go see the doctor. You be spitting up blood. That don't sound like no job for Miss Sarah. You go to see Miss Sarah when you have a cold. You need to go back to that doctor and do what they tell you. They got medicine they can give you. That's what happened to George Butler. He didn't go back to the doctor. You need to get another chest x-ray. Miss Sarah can't do that.

HEDLEY. Miss Sarah a saint. She a saint if ever God made one. She can heal anything. She got a big power. She got her roots. She got her teas. She got her powders. I wonder do she have a man? Maybe next time I ask her. A woman need a man. That's what Hedley say. I knock on your door last night.

LOUISE. You can knock all you want. You go knock on the doctor's door before you come knocking on mine.

HEDLEY. You know a woman need a man.

LOUISE. I don't need none that bad. I got me a thirty-two caliber pistol up there. That be all the man I need. You need to go see the doctor. It ain't like it was before. They letting the colored people in the sanitarium now. You can get help. They can make you well. You don't have to die from T.B.

HEDLEY. Everybody got a time coming. Nobody can't say that they don't have a time coming. My father have his time. And his father have his time. Hedley is fifty-nine years old. His time come soon enough. I'm not worried about that.

(CANEWELL enters. He is carrying a Golden Seal plant.)

CANEWELL. Who is this out here. Hey Louise. Hey Hedley... I started to bring my bible. I'm gonna bring it next time I come.

HEDLEY. "Ethiopia shall stretch forth her wings and every abomination shall be brought low."

CANEWELL. I ain't talking about that. I'm talking about ain't but a hundred and forty-four thousand people going to heaven. That's what it say in Revelations. Say one hundred and forty-four thousand of all the tribes of Israel shall be saved. All the rest gonna be cast into a fiery pit. Next time I'm going to bring my bible and show you.

LOUISE. Don't you all start that. What you got there?

CANEWELL. This is for Vera. This a Golden Seal plant. Ask Hedley about them. Hey Hedley tell her about the Golden Seal. Where's Floyd? Floyd here?

LOUISE. Don't get me to lying. He was out here with Vera. I don't know if he stay the night or not. I hope he didn't. She don't need to be getting tied back up with him. Not after that stuff he pulled.

CANEWELL. *(Calls.)* Hey, Floyd! Floyd! Get on out here man! They got some people from the neighborhood got together and went to see Miss Tillery about her rooster. They asked her to get rid of it cause it wake people up in the morning. She told them that's what it's supposed to do. They was still discussing the matter when I come on in here.

LOUISE. She need to get rid of it. This ain't the country, this the city. What she look like with that rooster?

CANEWELL. What you doing, Hedley? You fixing to kill some chickens?

LOUISE. If he start killing them chickens I'm going into the house.

HEDLEY. George Butler died. Hedley sell plenty plenty chicken sandwiches.

(HEDLEY exits into the cellar.)

CANEWELL. George Butler died? Every time I look up somebody's dying. If they ain't dying from one thing they dying from another. I done known six or seven men that got killed. That's why I say I wonder when's my time. Seem like I'm lucky to still be alive.

LOUISE. They be playing Floyd's record more and more. Everytime I turn around they be playing it. I got tired of hearing it.

CANEWELL. If he had listened to me he'd be a millionaire by now. Hey Floyd! Hey Schoolboy! I told Floyd if they put the record out it was gonna be a hit. They playing it all over. I told Floyd to get a cut of the money. They paid him a flat rate. I told him not to go for it. If he had listened to me he would be a millionaire by now.

(FLOYD comes to the window.)

FLOYD. What you doing all that hollering for?

CANEWELL. Get on out here, man!

FLOYD. I be there in a minute.

LOUISE. I hear you won a raffle down at the Loendi Club.

CANEWELL. I did. That's the radio I give Vera. That's a RCA Victor radio.

LOUISE. I hear you was supposed to win twenty-five dollars with it. Turn some of it loose. I need to buy some groceries.

CANEWELL. Where you hear that? Somebody lying to you. *(FLOYD enters from the house. CANEWELL sizes him up.)* Hey! Floyd "Schoolboy" Barton.

FLOYD. You see they playing the record? I told you! I told you the people would buy the record. I told you! They playing it everywhere.

CANEWELL. I know. I was the one who told you.

FLOYD. Naw. Naw. I knew it was gonna be a hit.

CANEWELL. I did too. I told you if they release it. I didn't know if they was gonna release it or not. I was sitting at home one day about two weeks ago and they played it. The first thing I say was, "I wonder if Floyd know."

FLOYD. Pitts come in the workhouse and told me. "Man, they playing your record." Time I looked around Mr. T.L. Hall was visiting me. All of a sudden he gonna invest some time in me.

CANEWELL. Time? He supposed to be your manager. Tell him to invest some money!

FLOYD. He told me to come down and see him this morning. He going to set everything up. Hey... look at this... I got a letter from the record company. Comeon we gonna go back up there and make another record. *(He shows CANEWELL the letter.)* You see that? They say, "Comeon, we'll work out the details when you get here!"

CANEWELL. I ain't going back up to Chicago.

FLOYD. It's gonna be different this time. We got a hit record.

CANEWELL. *You* got a hit record. You go on with it. I was up there and couldn't get back home. They arrested me for nothing. I ain't going back up there.

FLOYD. You don't have to be in Chicago for them to arrest you for nothing. They arrested me in Pittsburgh. I ain't done nothing but walk down the street. Come home from the cemetery after burying my mama, was walking down the street— and they arrested me. That ain't got nothing to do with Chicago. What's that got to do with Chicago?

CANEWELL. I ain't going back up there.

FLOYD. Mr. T.L. Hall gonna give us the money. It ain't gonna be like before

CANEWELL. Put me in jail. Couldn't get a job. I don't need all that. I ain't going back up there. They never get me back in the Cook County jail.

LOUISE. What you went to jail for? You ain't told us all that. You just say you didn't like it. What you went to jail for?

CANEWELL. Nothing. I ain't done nothing. Ask Floyd. *Singing.* That's all I did. I was right down there on Maxwell Street waiting on Floyd. I started fiddling with my harmonica. I said if I'm gonna stand here and play I may as well throw my hat down... somebody might put something in it. The police said I was disturbing the peace. Soliciting without a license. Loitering. Resisting arrest and disrespecting the Law. They rolled all that together and charged me with laziness and give me thirty days. I ain't going back up there.

LOUISE. I don't blame you. Where's Vera, Floyd?

FLOYD. She in the house getting ready to go to work. Comeon, Canewell, go over to the pawnshop with me. I got to see about getting my electric guitar out of pawn.

(HEDLEY enters from the basement.)

FLOYD. *(Sings.)*
"I thought I heard
Buddy Bolden say..."
HEDLEY. What he say?
FLOYD. He said, "Wake up and give me the money."
HEDLEY. Naw. Naw. He say, "Come here. Here go the money?"
FLOYD. Well... What he give you?
HEDLEY. He give me ashes.
FLOYD. Tell him to give you the money.

HEDLEY. Soon I going to be a big man. You watch. Buddy Bolden give me my father's money I'm going to buy a big plantation. Then the white man not going to tell me what to do.

FLOYD. He ain't gonna tell me what to do either, and I ain't gonna have no plantation. I don't need nothing but that .38. I was up there in the workhouse. The Captain say hurry... the Sergeant say run. I say if I had my .38 I wouldn't do neither one.

HEDLEY. I gonna be a big man.

LOUISE. You ain't gonna be nothing.

HEDLEY. The bible say it all will come to straighten out in the end. Every abomination shall be brought low. Everything will fall to a new place. When I get my plantation I'm gonna walk around it. I am going to walk all the way round to see how big it is. I'm gonna be a big man on that day. That is the day I dress up and go walking through the town. That is the day my father forgive me. I tell you this as God is my witness on that great day when all the people are singing as I go by... and my plantation is full and ripe... and my father is a strong memory... on that day... the white man not going to tell me what to do no more.

LOUISE. There ain't no plantations in Pittsburgh, fool! This the city.

HEDLEY. I'm gonna make one.

FLOYD. Hedley say he gonna make him a plantation.

CANEWELL. Hey, Hedley, what you gonna grow?

HEDLEY. I grow anything. Just like the white man. I grow tobacco. I grow oats. Anything.

CANEWELL. You ought to put you in some sugar cane.

HEDLEY. No. No sugar. I hate the sugar. Sugar beat many a man.

CANEWELL. That's how I got my name. My granddaddy used to cut sugar cane in Louisiana. Somebody seen him say, "That boy can cane well." Otherwise my name would be cottonwell.

HEDLEY. It's gonna be a big plantation.

FLOYD. I just want to come and sit on your front porch and drink Mint Juleps.

LOUISE. Look at Floyd signifying.

FLOYD. The man say he gonna get him a plantation. I ain't gonna be the one who tell him no. Somebody else gonna have to do that. If I see where he get his that might make me want to get one too.

CANEWELL. You should have heard Hedley night before last, Floyd. He was talking more stuff than a little bit. He was talking about Buddy Bolden... St. John the Divine... St. John the Revelator. St. Yolanda. Told me his Granddaddy was John the Baptist.

HEDLEY. I say he was baptized by a man call himself John the Baptist.

CANEWELL. We was talking about Zombies. Lazarus. Hey... hey, tell him, Floyd, Jesus ain't had no business raising Lazarus from the dead. If it's God's will then what he look like undoing it? If it's his father's work, then it's his father's business and he ought to have stayed out of it.

HEDLEY. His father will him to do it. Jesus is the Obedient Son of the Father. He was a black man, you know. The bible say his hair was like lamb's wool and his skin the color of copper. That's cause Mary was a Moabite.

CANEWELL. That ain't got nothing to do with Lazarus. What Mary being a Moabite got to do with Lazarus? I'm talking about you ain't supposed to go against nature. Don't care whether you the Son of God or not. Everybody know that. Lazarus even know that. When Lazarus was dying the second time... he was dying from pneumonia... somebody went up and got Jesus. Lazarus saw him coming and said, "Oh no, not you again!" See, all Jesus had done by raising him from the dead was to cause him to go through that much more suffering. He was suffering the pain of living. That's why the bible say you supposed to rejoice when somebody die and cry when they come into the world.

(VERA enters from the house. She has a man's hat in her hand.)

VERA. Is you all back on that again? Canewell, you left your hat here.

CANEWELL. I was wondering where my hat was. I thought it might be here. I was too embarrassed to come back and get it.

LOUISE. You ought to be embarrassed the way you all carried on.

FLOYD. What you doing with your hat at my house? You living dangerous.

VERA. It ain't your house. Let's get that straight first. If it's your house give me twenty-five dollars for the rent.

CANEWELL. They say wherever you hang your hat is your home. That just go to show you what a lie that is.

FLOYD. That's what I call home. If my hat's there, I'm gonna be there. What your hat doing in my house?

VERA. He left that hat here night before last. Him and Hedley sat out here talking about the bible and God knows what else. Sat here drinking that moonshine till they passed out. You know how Hedley get.

CANEWELL. I said I was gonna get crazy right with him. Ain't that right Hedley? We went tit for tat. Hey Vera, I bought you this Golden Seal plant. You plant that over there and that be all the doctor you need. That'll take care of everything you can think of and some you can't. You just take a pinch off of them leaves and make you a tea. Ain't that right. Hedley? Or else get you a little piece of the root.

HEDLEY. You have to plant it now. Don't let the roots dry out. The roots dry out easy.

(HEDLEY retrieves a shovel from beneath the landing and takes the plant from VERA. He begins digging in the flower garden.)

CANEWELL. Tell her, Hedley. That be all the doctor she need.

HEDLEY. My grandmother used to make a tea with the Golden Seal. She make a tea or she chew the leaves and rub it on her chest.

LOUISE. We ain't living back when your grandmother was living. You can go right across the street and see the doctor. Doctor Goldblum don't charge but two dollars. You can get some real medicine.

CANEWELL. This is real. Where you think Doctor Goldblum get his medicine from.

(VERA puts the plant into the hole HEDLEY has dug.)

HEDLEY. Watch you don't plant it too deep.

FLOYD. *(Puts his arms around VERA.)* What you planting that for? You ain't gonna be here to see it grow. We going to Chicago.

VERA. I ain't said nothing about going to Chicago.

CANEWELL. You trying to get Vera to go to Chicago and I'm looking to eat my breakfast in a brand new place.

LOUISE. I thought you was staying up there with Lulu Johnson.

CANEWELL. Naw I ain't up there no more. I'm drifting right now. But I ain't gonna be drifting long. I get me three rooms and a place to have a little garden and I'll be alright. Three rooms and a woman know how to sit with me in the dark and what else can a man want? If I was Rockefeller I could want for some more money... but other than that... what else could a poor man want?

LOUISE. Where you staying at if you ain't with Lulu Johnson no more?

CANEWELL. I'm staying down on Clark Street.

VERA. What you got on Clark street, Canewell?

CANEWELL. Nothing. I ain't got nothing.

VERA. Who you staying with?

CANEWELL. You don't know her. She just some old gal. I'm just helping her out with her rent. We got an understanding about what that is. It ain't nothing. I keep my trunk packed up.

VERA. That's what the problem is now. Everybody keep their trunk packed up. Time you put two and two together and try come up with four... they out the door.

FLOYD. The man said he got an understanding.

CANEWELL. Quite naturally when it's time for me to go... that be the end of our understanding. When it come to the end of our understanding I'm gonna drink a toast and keep on stepping.

FLOYD. Comeon, Canewell, I got to go downtown and get

my money first. They owe me thirty cents a day for working in the workhouse. That's ninety days worth of thirty cents. I'm gonna use that to get my guitar out the pawnshop.

VERA. You can go down there and pay on the light bill before they cut it off. And bring something back here if you wanna eat. Even people that have a hit record got to buy some groceries.

HEDLEY. You know why the pawnshop have a sign with three balls? Wherever you see a pawnshop you see them three balls. You ever notice that.

CANEWELL. Yeah... come to think of it. They all got three gold balls. Even if it ain't nothing but painted on it. What that mean?

HEDLEY. That mean the pawnshop man betting you three to one you not gonna get your stuff back.

(They ALL laugh. FLOYD exits into the house.)

VERA. How much it cost to go to Chicago?

CANEWELL. It was seventeen dollars and forty cents when me and Floyd went up there. That was last year. They might have put one of them yearly increases on it. Common sense say that can't last but so long if everything go up every year.

(FLOYD comes out of the house carrying a guitar.)

FLOYD. Hey, Canewell... remember this?

CANEWELL. That's that guitar you got off Odell.

FLOYD. I'm gonna carry this over to the pawnshop see what he give me for it. Then I wanna go over to the cemetery and visit my mother's grave. Vera, we be back. Joe Louis fighting tonight. Hey Hedley, Joe Louis fighting tonight.

HEDLEY. The Brown Bomber! Yes! The might Mighty Black Man!

(VERA, FLOYD and CANEWELL exit. HEDLEY kills a chicken as LOUISE retreats up the steps to her apartment. The lights go down on the scene.)

Scene 4

(The lights come up on the yard. It is several hours later. VERA and LOUISE are making food preparations.)

LOUISE. That's all I know. Ain't no telling what the truth of it is. My sister say it's best if she get away from there for awhile.

VERA. When she say she coming?

LOUISE. I got the letter but she didn't say. She didn't say what train or nothing. I pulled that mattress out I can lay it down on the floor. She ain't gonna be here long knowing her. With her little fast behind. I believe there's more to it than what they say.

VERA. Probably is. You don't never get the full story.

LOUISE. Talking about love. People don't know what love is. Love be anything they want it to be.

VERA. She might have been in love. Love don't know no age and it don't know no experience. You say she going on twenty-five. She might have been in love. Found somebody treat her half right.

What good it get her? She ain't got none of them now. She lucky she living. Who need that kind of love? One man in the ground and the other in jail. What she got? Went from two to sometime one to none to ducking and dodging bullets... for what? For love? No thank you I don't need me no love. I'm forty-eight going on sixty. Hedley's the closest I want to come to love... and you see how far that is.

VERA. Floyd want me to go to Chicago with him.

LOUISE. What for? So he can dog you around some more up there?

VERA. That's what I told him.

LOUISE. You can do better than that. Floyd don't mean nobody no good. He don't mean his own self no good. How he gonna mean you any good?

VERA. I believe Floyd means well. He just don't know how to do. Everything keep slipping out his hands. Seem like he stumble over everything.

LOUISE. However it go he make it go that way. He remind me of Henry. That man walked out on me and that was the best thing that happened to me. When he left I told myself say, "If you have to say hello before you can say good-bye... I ain't got to never worry about nobody saying good-bye to me no more." I ain't never going through one of them good-byes again. He was standing upstairs in the hallway. Told me say, "I'm leaving." I asked him, "What for? After twelve years. Why you gonna leave after all this time? After you done used me up." He say, "It's something I got to do." Then he went on and gathered up his things. He left a razor and a pair of shoes. They still up there.

VERA. That's like Floyd left his old guitar.

LOUISE. He got to the doorway and I told him, "Leave

your pistol. Don't leave me here by myself." He ain't said nothing. He took out his pistol and handed it to me. I told him, say, "I ought to shoot you." We laughed and then he kissed me good-bye. I ain't seen him since. I got that pistol upstairs now. What I'm trying to tell you is don't let no man use you up and then talk about he gotta go. Shoot him first.

VERA. Sometimes it seems like that more than they deserve.

LOUISE. Maybe you ought to go up to Chicago and find you a man.

VERA. Wouldn't that be something.

LOUISE. If you go up there with Floyd I give him six weeks and he be running around from this one to that one trying to keep you in the middle.

(FLOYD and CANEWELL enter the yard. FLOYD is still carrying his old guitar.)

FLOYD. These people around here is crazy. They don't know I ain't going for that. I go down there... the woman see I got the envelope. I ain't got no other piece of paper. She lucky I got that. I got other things to do then keep track of a piece of paper.

VERA. What piece of paper?

FLOYD. What kind of sense that make? She can see on the envelope they done sent me the letter to come down there. They told me that when I was in the workhouse. Say, "When you get out go down there." It ain't said nothing about no piece of paper.

VERA. What piece of paper?

FLOYD. She told me if I didn't have the paper I can't get

my money. I told her all that wasn't gonna change nothing. The government still owed me thirty cents a day for my time in the workhouse. I'm the one worked out there in the yard. They wasn't. She told me come back tomorrow. I'm gonna go down there. Cause they gonna give me my money. Paper or no paper they gonna give me my money.

VERA. What piece of paper?

CANEWELL. When Floyd was in the workhouse they sent him a letter. Say when you get out take this letter down to such and such a place and they will pay you thirty cents for however many days you was incarcerated. Floyd go down there and the woman asked him where the letter was. Floyd ain't had the letter... he just had the envelope. She told him they couldn't pay him unless he had the letter.

FLOYD. What kind of sense that make? Paper or no paper they still owe me the money. Now I got to go back down there tomorrow and straighten that out. I got to wait till tomorrow to get my electric guitar. I needed the money to get the guitar, and now I need the paper to get the money. That's supposed to give you a little starting place. Otherwise they could arrest me right now for vagrancy and give me another thirty days.

(RED CARTER enters. He is stylishly dressed.)

RED CARTER. I see you still back up in the alley.

FLOYD. Hey, Red.

LOUISE. Ohh. Just the man I want to see. Give me one of them Old Golds. Hedley give me one of these old Chesterfields. Here I'll trade you the pack.

RED CARTER. Naw. I ain't gonna do that. I don't want no Chesterfield! I don't see how people smoke them things.

FLOYD. Canewell said he wasn't gonna talk to you. You must have done something to him.

CANEWELL. I ain't said that. How you doing Red? I said I wasn't going to Chicago with you.

RED CARTER. Who going to Chicago? What Chicago? How you gonna be going with me when I ain't going my damn self. I ain't said nothing about Chicago.

FLOYD. Comeon, we going back up and make another record. They sent the letter to my sister's house.

RED CARTER. The record come out... I couldn't believe it. They started playing it on the radio. I told myself Floyd always did say it was gonna be a hit.

CANEWELL. I did too. I say if they released it.

FLOYD. Comeon, we going back up there.

RED CARTER. I don't know. Chicago a long way. It take the Greyhound round about fifteen hours. If I wanted to go that far I may as well visit my mama down in Opelika, Alabama. Down there where the women soft as cotton and sweet as watermelon.

FLOYD. They got some like that up there. They got some like that in Chicago. They got some of the prettiest women a man most ever seen. Comeon let's go back up there and make another hit record!

RED CARTER. They, do got some pretty women up in Chicago. Allright. Comeon let's go.

LOUISE. Red, you play bid Whist? We gonna play some cards after the fight. I'll let you be my partner. I bet we make a good team.

RED CARTER. You never can tell about nothing like that till after you try it.

LOUISE. Ain't that the truth.

VERA. Comeon, Louise... you gonna show me how you cook greens?

CANEWELL. You don't know how to cook no greens. *(CANEWELL begins following VERA and LOUISE as they exit the yard into VERA'S apartment.)* You get you about three pounds of turnips and about three pounds of mustard. I like to mix them together. Then you get you a big pot. Put some water in it. Cut the stems off the greens and throw that away. Tear the greens up into little pieces. Don't cut them. Some people cut them. That's where you mess up. Put you in a little piece... about a quarter pound of salt pork in there with them. Turn the fire way down real low and let them cook up about six hours. Throw you some red pepper seeds in there first. Cook that up and call me when it get done.

(LOUISE lets the screen door slam in CANEWELL'S face. RED CARTER takes out a cigar and hands it to FLOYD. Curing the following scene, the men set up the card table and chairs in preparation for the fight that evening.)

RED CARTER. Here.

FLOYD. What's that?

RED CARTER. What it look like? That's a cigar. Ain't you supposed to pass out a cigar when you have a baby? WillaMae done had another boy.

FLOYD. You ain't supposed to pass out this cheap-ass stuff.

RED CARTER. Here you go, Canewell.

FLOYD. You supposed to get you some of them dollar cigars.

RED CARTER. Joe Louis' daddy didn't pass out dollar cigars.

CANEWELL. Joe Louis' daddy ain't never seen no dollar cigar. Joe Louis's daddy was a poor man. I know you is too. But damn if they couldn't have been ten-cent cigars. One of them ten-cent King Edwards.

FLOYD. King Edwards don't cost but a nickel.

CANEWELL. I said one of them ten cent King Edwards. You not listening.

FLOYD. King Edwards don't cost but a nickel.

CANEWELL. That's the kind you know about. But you can buy some King Edward cigars that cost a quarter. Tell him, Red.

RED CARTER. They got some King Edwards cost fifty cents.

FLOYD. This cigar is stale.

RED CARTER. That's cause I been carrying it around with me for nine months.

FLOYD. How's WillaMae doing?

RED CARTER. She back at home now. That nine pound twelve ounces took a lot out of her but she handling it. Seem like he don't never stop eating. If I ate that much I wouldn't be able to get out the house. I wouldn't fit through the doorway. I wouldn't be able to get to the outhouse.

FLOYD. Hey Canewell, you remember that little rhyme about in days of old when knights was bold. I was trying to tell Red one time and couldn't think of it.

CANEWELL. "In days of old when knights was bold
and paper wasn't invented
They wiped their ass on a blade of grass—"

FLOYD and CANEWELL. "—And walked away contented!"

CANEWELL. But do you know this one?
"Ladies and gentlemen I stand before you to sit behind you

to tell you something I know nothing about—"

FLOYD. "The admission is free you pay at the door
There's plenty of seats you sit on the floor"

CANEWELL. "There's room for ladies but only men can go
And that's about all I know"

FLOYD and CANEWELL. "We're gonna discuss the four
corners of the round table!"

FLOYD. That always lay me out.

RED CARTER. Do you know...
"One bright morning in the middle of the night
Two dead boys got up to fight
Back to back they faced each other
Drew their swords and shot each other
A deaf policeman heard the noise
And came and killed those two dead boys."

CANEWELL." Watermelons sweet and green
Best watermelons you ever seen
You eat the meat
and pickle the rind
save the seed till planting time."

You know how to tell if a watermelon is sweet. You don't
thump them. You treat a watermelon just like you do a woman...
you squeeze them. If they soft they sweet. That's what my
daddy told me. I don't know if it's true or not about the watermelon. But I do know a soft woman is sweet. There is some
women you just melt right into them. I ain't talking about no
fat woman. But I do know something about that. There be
more woman there than any one man can handle.

FLOYD. There be a lot of them like that. Hard to handle.

RED CARTER. Where they at. I know how to handle them.
I used to have seven women. I tried to keep them separate and

give them all a day of the week. But that didn't work. I told one of them, "I'll see you on Tuesday. I got something to do Monday." She say, "Naw, Naw... I see you Friday night." I told the other one, " I'll see you on Thursday I got something to do Tuesday." She say, "Naw, Naw... I'll see you Friday." They all wanted to see me on Friday cause I was working. There was a time I couldn't get a woman. I go anywhere near a woman they get up and run. Time I got me a job I couldn't keep them off me. Women everywhere. All of a sudden I got right popular... except they all wanna see me on Friday. I tried to move my Friday woman over to Sunday but she got mad. My Sunday woman quit me and my Monday woman wanted to see me on Saturday. I got so confused I say the best thing for me to do was quit my job.

(Someone is heard approaching.)

    FLOYD. Who's that?
    CANEWELL. Ain't nobody but Hedley.
    FLOYD. Hey Red, watch this.

(HEDLEY enters. He has been out selling his eggs and chicken sandwiches. It has bee a good day, and his baskets are nearly empty.)

    FLOYD. *(cont. Sings.)*
    "I thought I heard
    Buddy Bolden say—"
    HEDLEY. What he say?
    FLOYD. He said, "Wake up and give me the money."
    HEDLEY. Naw. He say, "Come here. Here go the money."

FLOYD. What he give you?

HEDLEY. He didn't give me nothing.

CANEWELL. You tell him to give you the money. If he don't give it to you come and see me I'll cut him for you.

HEDLEY. I'll cut him myself.

RED CARTER. Here go a cigar.

HEDLEY. Yes! My cigar smoke better than your cigar.

RED CARTER. Naw, it don't smoke better than mine. You smoke a good cigar but it don't smoke better than mine.

CANEWELL. Red Carter got a baby boy.

HEDLEY. I hope he grow up and be big and strong like Joe Louis. Maybe one day I too have a son.

CANEWELL. Joe Louis fighting tonight. We gonna listen to it on the radio.

FLOYD. What you name him, Red?

RED CARTER. I ain't had the chance to name him nothing. She named him Mister.

CANEWELL. White folks gonna have a fit with a nigger named Mister. Mr. Mister Carter.

HEDLEY. Yes, the bible say Ethiopia shall rise up and be made a great Kingdom. Marcus Garvey say the black man is a king.

FLOYD. I don't want to hear nothing about no Bible.

RED CARTER. I'm with you Floyd. If I want to hear that I'd go to church.

FLOYD. God is in his heaven and he staying there. He must be up there cause a lot of things down here He don't know. He must not know about it. If He did it seem like He would do something about it. Being that He God and everything ain't right in his kingdom. Wouldn't you want everything to be right if you was God? So I figure He don't know about it. That's why I don't want to hear nothing about no bible. Ethiopia or nothing else.

HEDLEY. The black man is the conquering Lion of Judea you know. He like Toussaint L'Ouverture. He is the king! Most people don't know that. Hedley know. He know himself what blood he got. They say Hedley go on you too serious with that. But! Hedley know the white man walk the earth on the black man's back.

RED CARTER. Ain't nobody walking on my back. I ain't gonna let nobody walk on my back.

FLOYD. All I want is you to get out my way. I got somewhere to go. See everybody can't say that. Some people ain't got nowhere to go. They don't wanna go nowhere. If they wanted to go somewhere they would have been there. Time done got short and it getting shorter everyday. The only thing I want you to do is get out my way.

HEDLEY. You watch what Hedley say.

RED CARTER. Where them women go? I thought they was gonna cook something. I ain't had a cooked meal in so long.

FLOYD. What's wrong with that woman you got?

RED CARTER. Her mama ain't taught her how to cook. She know how to do everything else but she can't cook. At first I thought she was lying I come to find out it was the truth. I told her. "Come here baby I'm gonna show you this one time." Told her, "Pay attention." Then I showed her how to make biscuits. That's the only thing she can cook. That's why I'm getting fat. You hungry? We can go down there right now and get some biscuits.

FLOYD. You ought to teach her how to open up a can of beans. I don't want no woman who can't cook. She ain't too much good for me. She might be good for somebody but much as I like to eat she ain't good for me. That's what got me so mad when they arrested me cause I was gonna miss Vera's cooking. I asked the police say, "I done nothing. What you arresting me for?" He say, "I'm arresting you in advance. You gonna do something." I just look at him and told him, "Well, Boss you right cause if I had my druthers I'd cut you every which away but loose." He just laughed cause he know a black man ain't never had his druthers. They took me down there and beat me with them rubber hoses till I said Uncle. I told him say, "If I ever meet you out in the back by the alley one day we gonna have some fun." Give me ninety days for vagrancy.

RED CARTER. One time they arrested me for having too much money. I had more money than the law allowed. Must have... cause the police arrested me and put me in jail. Told me if I had that much money I must have stole it somewhere.

FLOYD. They got you coming and going. Put me in jail for not having enough money... and put you in jail for having too much money. Ain't no telling what they going to do next. *(FLOYD takes out his .38.)* That's why I got this here.

CANEWELL. That ain't gonna do nothing but get you arrested for carrying a loaded weapon.

FLOYD. You allowed to carry a loaded weapon you just can't hide it. You can carry it in your hand. That's your best bet. See you can carry it like this here and walk right on by the police. They can't do nothing to you. But even if you be carrying a empty pistol they can take and put you in jail for carrying a concealed weapon.

RED CARTER. Let me see that. That look like one of them thirty-eights.

FLOYD. That's a Smith and Wesson.

RED CARTER. *(Looks at gun.)* That's it. I used to have one just like that. I give it up for this snub-nose .32

(RED CARTER takes out his pistol and shows the pistol to FLOYD. HEDLEY exits into the cellar.)

FLOYD. I'd rather have that thirty-eight. This is nice but that got a bigger bullet.

CANEWELL. I don't need me nothing but this here.

(CANEWELL takes out an average size but thoroughly professional pocket knife.)

RED CARTER. What you gonna do with that.

FLOYD. Canewell cut him some people now. Everybody know that. There's a whole lot of niggers around here wearing Canewell's scars.

RED CARTER. Somebody go to cut me and I be done put four or five holes in him before he can draw back his arm.

CANEWELL. Naw. Naw. It don't work that way. There a lots of people think it work that way. And there a lot of people that used to think it worked that way. Most of them is in the graveyard. The ones that still think that way that's where they headed.

RED CARTER. That's cause they gun wasn't oiled. You keep your gun oiled and your trigger finger strong the only thing can beat you is a bigger or faster gun. You can't get beat with no knife. A knife ain't nothing but a piece of history. It's out of style.

CANEWELL. Cutting don't never go out of style. And you

don't have to depend on nobody for nothing. They quit making them bullets and ain't nothing you can do but try and beat somebody over the head with that hunk of metal.

RED CARTER. If you live long enough you just might find out.

(HEDLEY comes out of the cellar carrying a large butcher knife.)

FLOYD. What that you got?

CANEWELL. Hedley got his chicken knife. He a smart man. If it be me and him against you all... we'd win.

FLOYD. Naw. Naw. Not in Nineteen forty-eight. That's why we won the war. We had bigger guns. You can't fight with knives no more. They got the atomic bomb and everything.

RED CARTER. You don't need no atomic bomb. That ain't nothing but a big knife. This little .32 can handle that.

HEDLEY. But can you handle this.

(HEDLEY holds up a hot pepper.)

RED CARTER. What's that?

CANEWELL. Hedley got them peppers.

(HEDLEY pops one in his mouth and offers one to FLOYD.)

FLOYD. Naw... naw. You never get me to eat that. Give one to Red Carter. Hey Red, eat one of them peppers.

RED CARTER. It ain't nothing but a pepper.

(RED CARTER puts one in his mouth and almost chokes.)

CANEWELL. Hey Red, how many fingers I got up? Everything gonna stay like that for about a week.

(RED CARTER almost trips over Floyd's guitar.)

FLOYD. Watch it, Red. Watch it!

CANEWELL. Floyd have a fit if you trip over his guitar. Hey Red. Do I look like I'm made out of red glass?

FLOYD. I get my electric guitar. That will make me play better.

CANEWELL. Having a nice guitar don't make you play no better.

FLOYD. Not if you don't know how to play. But if you already know how to play good a nice guitar will make you feel better about yourself. If you feel better about yourself quite naturally you be able to play better. People see you with a nice guitar they know you put the music first. Even if you don't put the music first... it will work its way to the front. I know. I tried it many a time. I say, "Let me put this music down and leave it alone." Then one day you be walking along and the music jump on you. It just grab hold of you and hand on. Ain't too much you can do then.

CANEWELL. If I could put the music down I would have been a preacher. Many a time I felt God was calling. But the Devil was calling too and it seem like he call louder. God speak in a whisper and the devil shout.

RED CARTER. They say God have planned but the devil have planned also.

FLOYD. Yeah, well I'm planning too. I get that guitar. Mr. T.L. Hall give me the rest of the money and we be in Chicago making another hit record.

RED CARTER. You supposed to get my drums out the pawn.

FLOYD. Where you drums? I thought you had some drums. They told me you was raising all kind of hell down at the Workingmen's Club.

RED CARTER. That's when I had my drums. They in the pawnshop now.

FLOYD. They your drums.

RED CARTER. Tell him, Canewell. They my drums but it's his band. When the record come out it ain't gonna have my name on it. It ain't gonna have your name on it. It's gonna say "Floyd Schoolboy Barton". Just like the other one. If it have your name on it you supposed to take care of the band. Otherwise I don't need my drums. Let them stay in the pawnshop.

CANEWELL. That's right. That where Mr. T.L. Hall come in. Go down there and tell him your drummer need twenty-five dollars to get his drums out the pawnshop. Tell him my harmonica in there too. He supposed to be you manager. You supposed to pass the cost of running the band along to him.

FLOYD. The main thing is to get up to Chicago.

CANEWELL. I'll tell you this up front... *if* I go to Chicago. I say... *if* I go to Chicago. I want everything up front. It ain't gonna be like the last time. See bad luck and trouble try and follow me but I don't let it.

FLOYD. You ain't got to worry about nothing. Let me take care of it.

CANEWELL. I ain't gonna let nobody make no fool out of me.

RED CARTER. I ain't gonna let nobody make no fool out of me either. And I know you don't need to hear me say that twice.

FLOYD. That's all in Canewell's head. Ain't nobody making no fool out of him. That's the way the recording business work. You ain't gonna change that. The main thing is to get the record out here. Let the people hear it. Then come back and ask for more money. Then you can get double if it's any good. You can't be good just cause you say you is. The people got to hear it and want to buy it. That's what make you good. That's what I was trying to tell you when you walked out.

CANEWELL. I walked out cause the man didn't want to pay me what he said he was going to pay me. He didn't want to pay the agreed upon price. He wanna half way be in the liquor business. Twenty-five dollars and a bottle of whiskey do not make thirty-five dollars. He walked up and handed me the whiskey I took it cause I thought it was a present. Then he wanna charge me ten dollars for it. That ain't no way to do nobody.

RED CARTER. I ain't gonna work like that with me either. We may as well get this straight now. If he tell me thirty-five dollars that's what he gonna pay me.

CANEWELL. You see what I'm saying? I asked him say, "Is there any other kind of way we can do this?" He just looked at me. He told me "Leave." Just like that, "Leave." Just like you tell a dog "Sit". I told him "Bye!"

FLOYD. This time it's gonna be different. We gonna get the money up front.

CANEWELL. It wasn't all about the money. He treat me like he didn't care nothing about me.

FLOYD. He don't have to care nothing about you. You all

doing business. He ain't got to like you. Tell him Red, you got to take advantage of the opportunity. It don't matter if he like you or not. You got to take the opportunity while it's there.

CANEWELL. Just cause I was there on an opportunity don't mean he got to treat me bad. He on an opportunity too. You creating an opportunity for him.

FLOYD. The man ain't mistreated you. You all just had a misunderstanding. That could happen with anybody.

CANEWELL. I just say it ain't gonna happen with me no more.

RED CARTER. If he try to do that with both of us he gonna have double trouble.

FLOYD. You all ain't got to worry about that. Let me handle the business. Red. I'll get your drums out the pawnshop. I'll go get some more money from Mr. T.L. Hall.

CANEWELL. That's why I say I don't need nothing but this.

(CANEWELL takes out his harmonica and blows a few notes. FLOYD plucks the strings and starts to tune the guitar. RED CARTER takes out some drum sticks and drums on the table. The men begin to play. HEDLEY exits into the cellar.)

FLOYD. Let's see what we got here. *(Sings.)*
"God don't like it I know
Better quit drinking shine
God don't like it I know
Better quit drinking shine."

(HEDLEY enters from the cellar with a piece of 2x4, a hammer, a nail, and a piece of chicken wire. He slams the board

down and drives the nail in it, disrupting the music.)

FLOYD. *(Puzzled.)* What you doing Hedley?
HEDLEY. Watch!

(HEDLEY wraps the wire on the nail.)

CANEWELL. Hedley making him a one string. He say he
know something about music.
FLOYD. What he gonna do with a one string? He can't do
nothing with one string.
HEDLEY. Watch!
FLOYD. You can't do with that one string what I can do
with these six. Even if you can do something I bet you that it
be six times one. I make six times as much music.
HEDLEY. You watch. One string make plenty plenty mu-
sic. One string make plenty plenty music.
CANEWELL. Look out! Hedley say he make plenty plenty
music.
RED CARTER. Go ahead, Hedley. Look out, Floyd!
CANEWELL. I got a dollar on Hedley.
FLOYD. He can't top me with no one string.
CANEWELL. He ain't said he was gonna top you. He just
say he make plenty plenty music. You the one say you was
gonna top him.

*(HEDLEY finds a rock and puts it under the string to add
tension to the wire.)*

HEDLEY. Now. When I was a little boy I asked my Grand-
father where his mother was. He say she was long gone far

away. Say when he play this he could hear her pray. I asked him, "How?" He say, "Listen." *(He plucks the string.)* I didn't hear her. But I learned it and I used to sit and play and try to hear her. Once. Maybe. Almost.

(HEDLEY begins to play the instrument. It is a simple tune for a simple instrument. Really not much more than a piece of wire vibrating. The men listen hard.)

FLOYD. If I could hear my mother pray again I believe I'd pray with her. I'd be happy just to hear her voice again. I wouldn't care if she was cussing me out. They say you don't miss your water till you well run dry. If I could hear my mother's voice again I never would say nothing back to her. I wouldn't mind hearing her singing either. She used to do that some time. Used to sing "Old Ship of Zion." I believe that was her favorite. Though sometime she used to sing the "Lord's Prayer." I can still hear her singing... *(FLOYD sings.)*
"Our Father
which are in heaven
hallowed be thy name
Thy kingdom come
thy will be done
on earth as it is
in heaven.
Give us this day our daily bread
and forgive us our debts
as we forgive our debtors
Lead us not into temptation,
but deliver us from evil
for thine is the kingdom

and the power
and the glory
for ever
Amen."

RED CARTER. Where your mother buried at Floyd? My uncle's out in Greenwood.

FLOYD. That's where she at. She out there in Greenwood. I was out there today. Me and Canewell went out there. They got her buried over in the poor people part. Took me three hours to find the grave. They let the grass grow all over. I took and pulled up the grass and cleaned off her grave. Said I was gonna get her a marker. And that's what I'm gonna do. Cause when I leave this time I ain't planning on coming back. I get her that marker and I won't owe nobody nothing.

CANEWELL. They got everybody buried out there. They got George Butler buried out there. They got Jack Harding buried out there. Ed Weatherby. Uncle Doc and Aunt Lil. Raymond Polk. They got everybody buried out there in he poor section. You go out here and kill somebody they'll take him out there and bury him. Lightning come along and strike you and they'll take you out there and bury you right beside him. It don't matter what your dispute was. Death come along and say "Wham! Dispute that!" Death is fairer than life. He got a hundred seventeen men to do his bidding. He like the devil he ain't never satisfied. The devil get a hundred and seventeen men he want seventeen hundred and one more.

RED CARTER. But he do give you a chance. God don't give you no chances. The devil let you roll the dice. See if you crap out.

VERA. (*From her kitchen window.*) Hey Floyd! The fight's coming on.

(VERA puts her RCA Victor radio in the window. An announcer's voice is heard coming from the radio.)

ANNOUNCER. Good evening ladies and gentlemen. From Madison Square Garden it's Don Dunphy from ringside, where tonight Joe Louis, the Heavyweight Champion of the World, defends his title...

(As the lights dim, FLOYD helps VERA hang the lightbulb out from her window and LOUISE comes from the kitchen carrying a tray. The announcer's voice carries into the next scene.)

Scene 5

(The lights come up on the yard. The men have gathered closer to the radio so as to hear the fight better. VERA and LOUISE sit at the table which is covered with the evidence of food and drink.)

FIGHT ANNOUNCER. Louis sticks out a left—another left— a right to the head—and they tie up on the inside. The referee breaks them apart. Louis has been making good use of the jab. They're in the center of the ring now. Louis sticks out another jab and misses with a left hook. Conn grabs and hold. Conn throws a right to the body and a left to the head. Louis counters with a left hook—sticks out a jab and a right that grazes Conn's head. Conn retreats to the rope and Louis tries to pin him there but Conn punches his way out. Conn fires a hard right to Louis head. Louis backs up and Conn fires a hard right cross and tries to double on the left. Louis takes a step back, bobs and weaves and works his way on the inside and clinches. That punch hurt Louis. Conn tries to take advantage and fires a left and a right to the head. Louis is holding on as referee Marty Blaine breaks them apart.

FLOYD. Louis gonna get him.

FIGHT ANNOUNCER. Louis misses with a left, misses with a right. Conn with a hard left hook to Louis's head. He really wound up that time. Louis ducks a left and right and fires a right cross to the head. Another right. A right lead catches Conn high on the forehead as both men clinch, Louis back out, throws a left and a hard right that drops Conn to one knee.

HEDLEY. The black man hit hard you know.

FIGHT ANNOUNCER. The referee is counting over him. Conn appears to be alright as he takes a count of seven. He's on his feet. The referee wipes off his gloves. They're in mid ring. Louis fires a left and a right. A hard right a left and a straight right that knocks Conn down! He's flat on his back! His eyes are closed! It's all over! It's all over! Joe Louis has knocked out Billy Conn here in the eighth round!

(The men celebrate. They begin to circle the yard chanting "The Brown Bomber." RED CARTER grabs LOUISE and starts to dance with her. He pulls her to the center of the yard.)

RED CARTER. This is how you do the Joe Louis Victory Walk.

(RED CARTER begins to dance. CANEWELL and LOUISE

imitate him. CANEWELL stops and watches RED CARTER admiringly.)

CANEWELL. Look at Red. Yeah, he know how to do that.

RED CARTER. Comeon Vera I'll show you this. Then I'll show you the Joe Louis Shuffle. You know how to Jump Back?

VERA. I don't know all them little country dances.

RED CARTER. This dance is done all over the world. *(CANEWELL begins playing his harmonica.)* Follow me now. Do what I say. *(He puts his hand on his hip.)* Comeon now. Put your hand back. *(VERA puts her hand on her hip.)* Now just let it roll. You ain't got to worry about rocking it it'll rock by itself. *(Sings.)*

"Jump Jump Here
Jump Jump There
Jump Jump Jump
Everywhere
Jump Back Doo—ley
Jump Back Dooley when you really wanna blow your top..."

(RED CARTER jumps back and rolls his hip, in a subtle suggestive way.)

RED CARTER. *(Cont.)* See now this the way this go... each time you got to do better than me. Better than whoever you dancing with. You got to out do me. *(Sings.)*

"Jump Jump Here
Jump Jump There
Jump Jump Jump
Everywhere

Jump Back Doo—ley
Jump Back Dooley when you really wanna blow your top..."

(VERA begins to do the dance. It is suggestive and she loses herself in the science of it without realizing its full expression. Everyone watches RED CARTER and VERA dance. They kick up the dust. FLOYD broods. His brooding darkens the stage.)

RED CARTER. Go on shake it out.
LOUISE. Go Vera. That's right girl. Shake it.

(LOUISE urges her on. The matron's counsel. FLOYD grabs VERA by the arm and pulls her away.)

FLOYD. Look at Red trying to act like he know something. You can't dance, nigger. You lucky you can walk.

(The two men confront each other.)

RED CARTER. Yeah. The blind man stood on the road and cried. He couldn't see nothing.
FLOYD. I bet he can see this thirty-eight.
LOUISE. Hey... Hey... You all stop now.
RED CARTER. Stop what? Floyd knows better than to mess with me.
FLOYD. I ain't studying you.
RED CARTER. You got to be able to read to study me.
FLOYD. I can read well enough to read the coroners report. I know how to read D.O.A. I can read that.
CANEWELL. Comeon, Floyd...

LOUISE. You all come on now. You all gonna have to leave if you start all that arguing. I don't allow that around here. Come on let's play some cards. *(RUBY enters carrying a small suitcase. She is twenty-five. An uncommon woman. She exudes a sensuality that is electric. Everyone stops to look at her.)* Well look what the cat done dragged in. Child how come you ain't let somebody know when you was coming?

RUBY. I did. I sent the letter.

LOUISE. I got the letter last week. It ain't had no day no time no nothing. Just, "Aunt Louise, I'm coming." I know you can do better than that. ·

RUBY. I didn't know the time when I sent the letter. I had to wait till after Leroy's funeral. Then I had to wait till I could get the money.

LOUISE. Showing up unannounced on somebody doorstep like an orphan.

RUBY. I ain't no orphan.

LOUISE. That's her, Vera. That's who I was talking about.

RED CARTER. Do you need some help with your suitcase?

RUBY. I don't need no help. I done carried it this far. I needed some help at the bottom of the hill.

LOUISE. If you had told somebody when you was coming you wouldn't have had that problem.

(RUBY gets a pebble in her high heels and stumbles.)

RUBY. Got all these rocks around here.

LOUISE. Look at this old country gal with them fancy shoes complaining about rocks.

RUBY. I ain't country. Don't care where I come from. It's

all in how you act and I know I don't hardly act country. *(RUBY sits down and takes off her shoes.)* That's the longest hill I ever seen. I can't be walking up these hills getting all them muscles in my legs.

CANEWELL. For your information, in case you ain't figured it out yourself, this here is called the Hill District. That one of two things a woman coming into Pittsburgh need to know. The other thing is how to find me. My name is Canewell and you can find me right down there on Clark Street. That's the same Clark like the candy bar. That's down in what the people call Little Haiti. Just ask anybody where Canewell lives and they will tell you.

RED CARTER. Naw... don't pay him no mind. My name Red Carter but sometimes people just call me Red. You can call me anything you want to. What you say your name was?

RUBY. My name is Ruby. I need me some water.

LOUISE. Go on in the house and get some. There's some in the house.

RUBY. Is it cold?

LOUISE. Go on in there and find out.

RUBY. Where to go?

LOUISE. Up them steps to the third floor. The door on the left. Don't go on the right. That's where Hedley live. Just go on up there.

(RUBY starts up the stairs. CANEWELL goes after her suitcase.)

CANEWELL. Here... I'll help you with this.

(RED CARTER grabs hold of the suitcase at the same time as CANEWELL.)

CANEWELL. Watch yourself, Red!
RED CARTER. You watch yourself!
CANEWELL. I was here first!

(The two men start at each other. RED CARTER gradually lets go of the suitcase. RUBY takes the suitcase from Canewell and goes up the stairs.)

LOUISE. Comeon let's play some cards. Let's play some whist. Red you said you'd be my partner. Comeon Floyd.

(LOUISE starts to clear the table.)

RED CARTER. Naw, I changed my mind. I'll watch the first one.
LOUISE. Comeon Hedley. You and Floyd play me and Vera. Comeon, Vera. Deal the cards.
FLOYD. I'll deal. I don't trust you all. You liable to deal from the bottom of the deck.
VERA. We don't care if you deal. Go on deal them.
RED CARTER. Where your niece from, Louise?
LOUISE. Birmingham. My whole family is from Birmingham.
FLOYD. You ready, Hedley. Let's show them.
HEDLEY. If you going to play. Let's play.
RED CARTER. How long she staying?
LOUISE. I don't know. Knowing her and her little fast behind she ain't gonna be here long.
CANEWELL. Louise I didn't know you had no nieces.
LOUISE. There's a whole lot of things you don't know.
CANEWELL. I guess you right about that.

LOUISE. We gonna beat you next. You and Red Carter.

FLOYD. Your bid, Louise.

LOUISE. Two.

HEDLEY. Three.

VERA. Four.

FLOYD. Pass.

VERA. Clubs.

(RED CARTER sits beside LOUISE looking on at her hand.)

FLOYD. Now here's what I don't understand. If I go out there and punch a white man in the mouth they give me five years even if there ain't no witnesses. Joe Louis beat up a white man in front of a hundred thousand people and they give him a million dollars. Now you explain that to me.

RED CARTER. He got a license and you don't. He's registered with the government and you ain't.

FLOYD. What's trumps?

VERA. Clubs.

FLOYD. Who say it's clubs?

VERA. I do. That's what I bid. You said pass. Where you been. Come to the table.

LOUISE. It don't matter to me what it is. I can play on all of them.

HEDLEY. Whoa! Watch it! Watch it! No talking about your hand!

FLOYD. I just asked what trumps was. I can play on them too.

LOUISE. Floyd ain't got his mind on the game.

VERA. I know.

LOUISE. Vera, you selling Mother's Day flowers this year?

VERA. Yeah, if Floyd get me some crêpe paper.

CANEWELL. I'll get you some. What you want... red and white?

VERA. Three rolls of red and three rolls of white. And one roll of green tape.

CANEWELL. I'll get it for you tomorrow.

(The rooster crows. The duck quacks.)

FLOYD. If I had me a BB gun I'd shoot that rooster. That be a warning to the duck.

LOUISE. Ain't that the truth. She don't need that rooster. All she got to do is go down to Woolworths and get her an alarm clock. It don't cost but a dollar and forty-nine cents.

CANEWELL. That's one of them Alabama roosters. See, he fall in love with the way he sound and want to crow about everything. Everytime the notion strike him. That don't do nothing but get people confused. That kind of rooster ain't no good for nobody. Best thing you can do is try and make a stew out of him. If you wanna take the time to fuss with it. Then you got your Georgia rooster. It don't know it's a rooster. It thinks it's a dog. It crow everytime somebody come around. It don't do nothing but make the bull dog mad cause it's trying to put him out of a job. Then you got you Mississippi rooster. He sit up on the roost and roost. The sun even act like it wanna come up he be right there with it. The sun come up at five he crow at 5:01. Seem like he say let me do this a get it over with so I can get back to roosting. He take his job real serious but he don't want to be working all day. He say I crow once in the morning and twice on Sunday. Let you know when it's time to go to church. That's the only time he crow other than if somebody disturb the hens in the barnyard. That's the way your Mississippi rooster is.

VERA. Canewell, where you get all this stuff from?

CANEWELL. I just know it. I know lots of things. I'll tell you another thing about the rooster. The rooster didn't crow during slavery. He say, "Naw. I ain't gonna be part of nothing like that. I ain't gonna wake nobody up." He didn't start crowing again till after the Emancipation Proclamation. The people got to whooping and hollering so. He say, "Naw. You all ain't gonna leave me out." That's why the crow so loud. If you think I'm lying go and find you somebody from back in slavery time and ask them if they ever heard the rooster crow.

LOUISE. Come on, Vera. We got them. We got them now.

FLOYD. Canewell talking about that rooster distracted me. He don't know nothing about no Alabama rooster.

CANEWELL. You can tell. He ain't no Mississippi rooster. Mississippi roosters crow at five o'clock. I bet he don't even wake up tlll about eight.

FLOYD. How you know what time he wake up?

CANEWELL. I can hear him from over where I live.

FLOYD. You can't hear that rooster. I bet you five dollars you can't hear him down there.

CANEWELL. Well you can't hear him but you can hear him just same. You know there's a rooster crowing.

VERA. Comeon, Floyd... play if you gonna play. You holding up the game with that. Don't nobody care where that rooster's from or how loud he can crow.

LOUISE. Wherever he from... he in Pittsburgh now. This the city. Roosters belong in the country. If they belong anywhere. Miss Tillery need to get rid of that thing.

HEDLEY. The rooster is the king of the barnyard. He like

the black man. He king.

VERA. Comeon Hedley. It's your turn. Louise played a five.

FLOYD. They don't have all that in Chicago. You ain't gonna find no rooster living next to you making all that noise in Chicago.

CANEWELL. There's more roosters in Chicago than there is in Pittsburgh. There's more people from the country in Chicago then there is in Pittsburgh.

RED CARTER. You right. There ain't nothing but niggers from Mississippi in Chicago. The 61 highway run straight to Chicago. That 61 highway is the longest highway in the world... run straight North to Chicago. That 61 highway wore many a man out. That 61 highway—

CANEWELL. We ain't talking about no highway. We talking about how many roosters they got in Chicago.

RED CARTER. That's what I'm saying. That 61 highway run straight out of Mississippi.

CANEWELL. There's too many people up there for me. I don't see how nobody get to know nobody.

FLOYD. There's more people and there's more things to do. More people mean more opportunity. But see you don't know how to take advantage of opportunity. You don't know nothing about that.

CANEWELL. I know I ain't gonna stay up there.

FLOYD. Stay here then! I can get me a harmonica player. They got harmonica players on every corner of Chicago.

CANEWELL. They ain't got none like me. You gonna find that out.

(The rooster crows.)

FLOYD. Stop all that noise!

(FLOYD gets up and throws a stone across the fence.)

VERA. Floyd! Don't be throwing nothing over there!

(HEDLEY suddenly gets up from the table and starts to exit the yard.)

LOUISE. Hedley sit back down there... where you going? Comeon and finish this hand.

(HEDLEY doesn't answer. He exits the yard.)

FLOYD. What's the matter with him?
VERA. You know how he gets. I don't know why you wanna do something to get him agitated.
FLOYD. What I do? I ain't done nothing to nobody. Comeon, Canewell, take Hedley's hand. Let's beat them.

(The rooster crows.)

RED CARTER. He do sound like a Alabama rooster.
LOUISE. Where you from, Red?
RED CARTER. I was born in Alabama. I was born in the country. Most people don't know that. They think I was born in the city cause I got city ways.

(The rooster squawks. RUBY enters from the upstairs.)

CANEWELL. Hey, Ruby. Comeon... you play whist? If

you don't play no whist. I'll play whatever you play if it ain't nothing but pitty-pat.

RED CARTER. Comeon. You can be my partner. Get up, Canewell.

LOUISE. You all leave her alone now. She just got here.

CANEWELL. Do you gamble? I'm looking for a gambling woman.

RUBY. Ain't nobody gonna do no gambling. You have to gamble by yourself.

FLOYD. Here you go, baby. You can have my seat. My name's Floyd. Floyd "Schoolboy" Barton.

RUBY. I don't want to play no cards. I don't see why people play cards noway. You ain't doing nothing but wasting time.

(HEDLEY enters the yard carrying the rooster.)

HEDLEY. You want or you don't want, it don't matter. God ain't making no more roosters. It is a thing past. Soon you mark my words when God ain't making no more niggers. They too be a done thing. This here rooster born in the barnyard. He learn to cock his doodle do. He see the sun, he cry out so the sun don't catch you with your hand up your ass or your dick stuck in your woman. You hear this rooster you know you alive. You be glad to see the sun cause there come a time sure enough when you see your last day and this rooster you don't hear no more. *(He takes out a knife and cuts the rooster's throat.)* That be for the living. Your black ass be dead like the rooster now. You mark what Hedley say. *(He sprinkles the blood in a circle.)* This rooster too good live for your black asses. *(He throws the rooster on the ground.)* Now he good and right for you.

(HEDLEY exits the yard. Everyone is stunned.)

FLOYD. What he do that for? Hey Hedley... what you kill the rooster for?

VERA. Comeon leave him alone. He ain't right.

FLOYD. Hey, Hedley! Hey! What you do that for?

(The lights go down on the scene.)

END OF ACT ONE

ACT II

Scene 1

(the lights come up on HEDLEY in the yard. FLOYD'S record, "That's All Right," plays on the radio in the house. HEDLEY has turned his table into a grill and has just finished cooking several chicken breasts. He is making sandwiches and wrapping them in wax paper. He places the sandwiches inside his wire basket which is filled with hard boiled eggs, cigarettes and candy bars. He wears a long leather apron. RUBY enters. She watches HEDLEY for a moment.)

HEDLEY. *(Sings.)*
"I thought I heard
Buddy Bolden say
Soon I be a big man someday..."

RUBY. What you got in them baskets? Is them eggs? Let me have one of them eggs. *(HEDLEY takes an egg out of the basket and gives it to her.)* You ain't got no salt do you? *(HEDLEY shakes his head no.)* I don't know what I want no salt for anyway. Salt killed my daddy. —What you kill that rooster for?

HEDLEY. Cause nobody want him.

RUBY. I don't understand. He ain't done nothing to nobody. That's just like Leroy. He ain't done nothing to nobody

71

either. Now if it had been a mean old dog that was going around biting everybody he's liable to live forever. Nobody ain't gonna do nothing to him.

HEDLEY. *(Sings.)*
"I thought I heard
Buddy Bolden say..."

(RUBY walks around the yard. HEDLEY watches her with undisguised lust.)

HEDLEY. *(cont. singing.)*
"Soon I be a
Big man someday..."

RUBY. Can you put them feathers in a mattress? I should have you make me a mattress. Make it soft and low.

HEDLEY. Go on, girl How he to know it soft and low unless he try it. I can make you anything you want. Just be sure you want it.

RUBY. I need me a mattress.

HEDLEY. *(Sings.)*
"I thought I heard
Buddy Bolden say..."

RUBY. Who is Buddy Bolden?

(HEDLEY busies himself with his work as he talks.)

HEDLEY. It is who my father name me after. King Buddy Bolden.

RUBY. My mother named me after my grandmother. Grandma Ruby. She say she started to name me after her cousin Bertha. Why your father name you that?

HEDLEY. My father play the trumpet and for him Buddy Bolden was a God. He was in New Orleans with the boats when he make them run back and forth from Haiti to New Orleans. The trumpet was his first love. He never forgot that night he heard Buddy Bolden play. Sometime he talked about it. He drink his rum, play his trumpet, and if you were lucky that night he would talk about Buddy Bolden. I say lucky cause you never see him like that with his face light up and something be driving him from inside and it was a thing he love more than my mother. That is how he names me, King... after King Buddy Bolden. It is not a good thing he named me that. (Pause.) I killed a man once. A black man. I am not sorry I killed him.

RUBY. What you kill him for? Elmore killed Leroy for nothing.

HEDLEY. He would not call me King. He laughed to think a black man could be King. I did not want to lose my name so I told him to call me the name my father give me and he laugh. He would not call me King and I beat him hard with a stick. That is what cost me my time with a woman. After that I don't tell nobody my name is King. It is a bad thing. Everybody say Hedley crazy cause he black. Cause he know the place of the black man is not at the foot of the white man's boot. Maybe it is not alright in my head sometimes. Cause I don't like the world. I don't like what I see from the people. The people is too small. I always want to be a big man. Like Jesus Christ was a big man. He was the son of the Father. I too. I am the son of my father. Maybe Hedley never going to be big like that. But for himself inside. That place where you live your own special life. I would be happy to be big there. And maybe my child, if it be a boy, he would be big like Moses.

I think about that. Somebody have to be the father of the man to lead the black man out of bondage. Marcus Garvey have a father. Maybe if I could not be like Marcus Garvey then I could be the father of someone who would not bow down to the white man. Maybe I could be the father of the messiah. I am fifty nine years old and my times is running out. Hedley is looking for a woman to lie down with and make his first baby. Maybe... maybe you be that woman for me. Maybe we both be blessed.

RUBY. You old enough to be my father. I ain't hardly thinking about no messiah. You need to put all that stuff out of your mind. You too old to be having babies anyway.

(HEDLEY exits into the cellar. FLOYD come into the yard through the gate.)

FLOYD. Hey, Ruby. How you doing? *(FLOYD goes into VERA'S. He returns carrying his guitar case.)* Ruby, I thought you'd be gone. Be out looking around the city. See where you at.

RUBY. I know where I'm at. I know I'm in Pittsburgh. I done seen lot of cities before. They may not have been up North but a city is a city. It don't make no difference.

FLOYD. Sure it do. This is Pittsburgh. This ain't Alabama. Some things you get away with up here you can't get away with down there. I'll show you around. It ain't as good as Chicago but you be surprised at what you find. Comeon don't worry about nothing... I'll tell everybody you my cousin.

RUBY. You gonna buy me a beer?

FLOYD. I'll buy you a beer and anything else you want. Comeon.

(HEDLEY enters with boxes of candy and glares at FLOYD.)

RUBY. Wait, I got to go change my shoes.

(RUBY exits upstairs.)

FLOYD. Hey, Hedley. Is you feeling better today?
HEDLEY. I feel fine.
FLOYD. Did you wake up on time... that's the question.

(HEDLEY ignores FLOYD'S joke.)

HEDLEY. I thought you had something to do. You was in a
big rush this morning. I thought you went to the pawnshop to
get your electric guitar?
FLOYD. Don't say nothing to me about no guitar. You
gonna get me started. I go over there to get my guitar and the
man tell me I'm two days late. My ticket expired. It wasn't
good but for ninety days. He didn't give me but ten dollars on
the guitar and now he want to sell it back to me for fifty dollars. I told him it wan't gonna work that way. Seeing as how I
was in the workhouse all that didn't count. They don't know I
ain't going along but so far. Then I'm through with it. When
I'm through with it there be more hell to pay than the devil got
ways to count. I'm gonna take the pawnshop man this guitar
and lay ten dollars on top of that. If he don't want to go along
with that I'm gonna see if he go along with my .38.
HEDLEY. The white man got a big plan.

(HEDLEY busies himself with his baskets.)

HEDLEY. *(cont. singing.)*
"I thought I heard Buddy Bolden say,
Here go the money, King take it away."
FLOYD. Broke as I am I need to have Buddy Bolden bring me some money. I'd take it away. I'd tell him, "Wake up and give me the money."
HEDLEY. No. No. He say, "Come here, here go the money."
FLOYD. That's what I'm talking about. I need to have somebody say that to me. Bad as I need some money. I wouldn't care who it was. Buddy Bolden or anybody else. High John the conqueror. Yellow Jack. Brer Rabbit. Uncle Ben. It could be anybody.
HEDLEY. It is my father's money. What he send to me. He come to me in a dream. He say, "Are you my son?" I say, "Yes Father I am your son." He say, "I kick you in the mouth?" I say, "Yes, Father, I ask you why you do nothing and you kick me." He say, "Do you forgive me?" I say, "Yes, Father, I forgive you." He say, "I am sorry I died without forgiving you your tongue. I will send Buddy Bolden with some money for you to buy a plantation so the white man not tell you what to do." Then I wait and I wait for a long time. Once Buddy Bolden come and he say, "Come here, here go the money." I go to take it and it all fall like ash. Ashes to ashes and dust to dust. Like that. It all come to nothing.
FLOYD. He coming back. And he gonna give you the money. He got to give it to you. What else he gonna do with it? He gonna give it to you and lay the interest on top of it. You liable to buy two plantations. *(RUBY enters from the stairs.)* Is you ready? Comeon. *(RUBY starts to exit the yard.)* I'm gonna follow you wherever you go.

(FLOYD follows after RUBY. HEDLEY grabs FLOYD by the arm with a great sense of urgency.)

HEDLEY. You are a king! They look at you and they say this one... this one is the pick of the litter. This one we have to watch. We gonna put a mark on this one. This one we have to crush down like the elephant crush the lion! You watch your back! The white man got a big plan against you. Don't help him with his plan. He look to knock you down. He say, "That one!" Then they all go after you. You best be careful!

(The lights come down on the scene.)

Scene 2

(The lights come up on VERA and LOUISE in the yard. VERA is making red and white flowers from crêpe paper.)

LOUISE. Julie gave me that dress. You know that red dress. It's too small for me. You ought to try it on.

VERA. I can't get in that dress.

LOUISE. You ought to try it on. It might fit you. I hate to see it go to waste.

VERA. Maybe it'll fit Ruby.

LOUISE. I'll let her try it on, but she's gonna take her little fast behind out here and get her a job. I ain't gonna be taking care of her. They need anybody down there where you are? She know how to dust.

VERA. I can ask and see. I might just go on up to Chicago.

LOUISE. You can do what you want to do and I wouldn't be one to try and tell you not to do something. I just know even though it seem like Floyd know how to do the right thing... he really don't. Floyd is the kind of man can do the right thing for a little while. But then that little while run out.

VERA. I can always come back. The way he talk about it do make you want to see it. Just to see if it's like he say. Maybe I can be a different person up there.

LOUISE. Wherever you go you got to carry you with you. You ain't gonna all of a sudden be a different person just cause you in a different city. You can put that out your head right now. (RUBY enters. She has a letter in her hand.) Where you been?

RUBY. I been with Floyd. He took me over on the Northside then he took me down the Workingmen's Club and introduce me to some people. He was telling everybody I was his cousin. One man wanted to take me to Harlem.

LOUISE. Them rogues down there can't take you around the corner. Talking about Harlem.

VERA. Where's Floyd?

RUBY. He went back over to the pawnshop with Canewell. We went over there this morning and the waterline broke. They had the whole street blocked off. The pawnshop was closed. They say they was gonna get it fixed and be open this afternoon.

LOUISE. What's that you got?

RUBY. My mother sent me a letter from Elmore. He had the nerve to write me. I can't stand no jealous man.

LOUISE. All men are jealous. Especially if you make them that way.

RUBY. I ain't done nothing to make him jealous. He was

always like that. He was jealous when I met him. He don't know that just make you wanna leave him quicker. He trying to hold onto you and end up driving you away. Elmore started to get mean so I left him. Everybody seen me and Leroy together and knew I had quit Elmore. I told Leroy Elmore was jealous of him. He say he didn't care. Say he still loved me. Asked me who did I love. I told him the truth. I didn't love neither one of them. They both was nice in their own way. Then they got into a fight. I tried to tell them Ruby don't belong to nobody and Ruby ain't gonna take but so much of anybody. After the fight I saw Elmore and he asked me where Leroy was. Say he wanted to go make up. I told him Leroy was at the barber shop and he went up there and shot him before Leroy could have a chance to say anything. The problem with Elmore was he never could get enough of me. He used to tell me he wanted to take it all so nobody else could have me. He wasn't gonna leave none for nobody else to hear him tell it. That make you feel funny to be with a man want to use you up like that.

LOUISE. He don't mean you no good. That's for sure.

VERA. That when they say they got blood in their eyes for you. I tell them if you got blood in your eye then you can't see good. What I want with a blind man.

RUBY. It was never enough for him. We lay down at night. In the morning. In the afternoon. Just stop what you doing... if you doing anything. Even that don't be enough. I told him one time say, "Baby look in the mirror and count that as twice."

LOUISE. You sound like you complaining. You hear this Vera. Child I can think of ten women be happy to have a man look at them twice. They get mad if he get tired.

VERA. I'd rather that than to have somebody try to abuse you like that. They ain't loving you they using you.

RUBY That's what I'm trying to say.

LOUISE. I wonder what he using now. How much time he get?

RUBY. The judge told him he was gonna throw the book at him. He had the nerve enough to tell me to wait on him. He don't know I'm pregnant.

LOUISE. He ain't the only one don't know. Whose baby is it? Elmore's or Leroy's?

RUBY. I don't know. I got to wait to find out. I hope it's Leroy's.

(FLOYD and CANEWELL enter the yard.)

CANEWELL. Hey, Vera, you all can bust out them dresses you all got stuffed in the closets.

FLOYD. We went down to the Blue Goose with Mr. T.L. Hall and he arranged everything for us to play at the Mother's Day Dance.

CANEWELL. Told Floyd they was gonna give him an advance tomorrow. Say they was gonna give him half the money up front. And... tell them Floyd!

FLOYD. Ask Canewell... we got a date for the recording studio in Chicago!

CANEWELL. June 10th. At ten o'clock in the morning!

FLOYD. Mr. T.L. Hall showed me the letter he got from the record company. Say be there on June 10th to make some more records. Said they were... what they say Canewell...

CANEWELL. Enthusiastic.

FLOYD. That's it... said they were enthusiastic about the prospect!

VERA. That's nice, Floyd.

FLOYD. Comeon, Vera you got to go up there with me. I ain't going up there by myself. Canewell say he going. You can't say no to a man with a hit record.

CANEWELL. I told Floyd I ain't gonna stay but long enough to make the record. There's too many people up there for me. So many people you can't even walk down the street. I ain't gonna stay but long enough to make the record.

FLOYD. We ain't talking about how long you staying. Nobody care how long you staying.

LOUISE. I can't remember the last time I was down the Blue Goose. Vera you ought to come down the shop and let me do your hair.

FLOYD. I went over to the gravestone man and ordered my mother a marker for her grave.

CANEWELL. He picked out a real nice one. Got two roses engraved on either side of it. It look real nice.

FLOYD. I give him that twenty-seven dollars plus the five dollars I got for selling my old guitar. He say he would try to have it ready by Mother's Day.

(HEDLEY enters the yard with his baskets still half full of cigarette boxes, loose candy bars, and a sandwich or two. He is angry. He clutches a letter in his hand.)

HEDLEY. Hedley don't go nowhere! *(He flings one of his baskets across the yard. He crosses to LOUISE and stands in front of her. He slowly balls up the letter and throws it down.)* Hedley don't go nowhere! My father... he take care of the horses. He take care of the horses for the shoemaker. He take care of the horses for the baker. He take care of the horses for the doctor! *(He flings the other basket across the yard.)* He go hungry... with no bread from the baker. He walk with nothing but the tops of his shoes... nothing from the shoe maker. He die while he wait for the doctor to come! All his life he taking care for the shoemaker, he taking care for the baker, he taking care for the doctor. He get sick. My mother call for the doctor. Three days later the doctor come. She tell him "I thought you was the undertaker. He died two days ago." He say, "Can I pray?" She tell him, "No." That's what I tell you, "No." (HEDLEY stomps on the letter and grinds it into the ground with his foot.) The white man cannot help me! It is a plot against the black man! Hedley don't go nowhere! Hedley don't go nowhere!

(HEDLEY exits up the stairs. Every one looks at LOUISE for an explanation. LOUISE picks up the letter and looks at it.)

LOUISE. Hedley got T.B. and don't want to go into the sanitarium. He got that letter from the board of health telling him to be down there on Thursday. I called down there and told them. They want him to come down and get tested.

CANEWELL. They letting colored in the sanitarium now. They got one right up there on Bedford. They moved all the white people out and it's sitting there half empty. They looking to fill it up. He ought to go on and let them take him. He can get well.

VERA. That's what Louise tried to tell him.

LOUISE. He talking all this plot against the black man stuff. You know how he is.

CANEWELL. Everything is a plot against the black man to Hedley.

FLOYD. Hedley say he don't want to go. He got a right for nobody not to tell him what to do. If it was me I wouldn't go either.

CANEWELL. Least he can get well. Everybody don't always have that choice. He lucky. A whole bunch done died without a chance to get well. He one of the lucky ones. He can choose whether he want to live or die.

FLOYD. Then let him choose! He say he don't trust it. How you gonna trust it for him. He know what the stakes are.

VERA. Hedley don't know he can get well. He don't believe it. Louise tried to tell him. He living too far in the past.

FLOYD. Then let him find out. If he don't know he'll find out. He say the white man can't help him, that's a choice he's making. You can't make it for him. Let him find out the error of his ways. If he don't know the consequences he's gonna find out the truth. Hedley know who he is. He know what he think of himself. And he knows what he think of the white man. It might not be what you think but you ain't him. You ain't been where he been. You ain't been...

HEDLEY enters. He walks quickly down the stairs. He has put on a coat and hat. He quickly exits the yard. Everyone watches him as the lights go down.)

Scene 3

(The lights come up on the yard. FLOYD is alone in the yard pacing. CANEWELL enters. FLOYD looks at him and continues pacing.)

FLOYD. I went over to the pawnshop to meet Mr. T.L. Hall and he didn't show up. I went downtown and ain't nobody seen him. He usually be down there sitting around that hotel. Ain't nobody seen him down there. Didn't he say meet him over at the pawnshop at nine o'clock?

CANEWELL. That's what he said.

FLOYD. I can't be playing around. He got the advance from the Blue Goose. He supposed to give me that and get my guitar out the pawnshop.

CANEWELL. It say on the radio that we gonna be down at the Blue Goose on Sunday.

FLOYD. I can't play down there unless I have my guitar.

CANEWELL. That's what I'm saying. They blasting it all over town that you gonna be down the Blue Goose playing the Mother's Day Dance. Say Floyd "Schoolboy" Barton with his hit record "That's All Right" and you ain't even got a guitar.

FLOYD. Mr. T.L. Hall told me say "Be on time." I was over there five minutes to nine. I can't be playing around. I still got to get Red's drums out the pawn. And you heard me tell the gravestone man I'd be back with the rest of the money.

CANEWELL. Did you look in the Brass Rail by the courthouse? Sometime he be sitting in there with a bunch of other white men. Either that or the Oyster House.

FLOYD. I looked in the Brass Rail. I didn't look in the Oyster House. If I knew where he lived I'd go over to his house.

CANEWELL. They don't like that. They don't like you coming over to their house.

FLOYD. That's what makes me mad. He told me to meet him down there this morning so we could go over the details. I got to get Vera a dress to wear down the Blue Goose. If she gonna go with me she supposed to look like her man got a hit record.

CANEWELL. Her man got a hit record but he ain't got no hit record money. If you had listened to me...

FLOYD. I'm tired of hearing that. It's cause of you that I only got one record out. If you hadn't walked out of the recording session I'd have four or five records. I should have kicked your ass for walking out. I still might not have nothing but I'd have my satisfaction. You always talking about if I had listened to you. What you got?

CANEWELL. I got the same as you... but I ain't you. I ain't got my name on a hit record. You supposed to have. You supposed to have the Buick you talking about. You supposed to have that guitar... Red Carter's drums and some money in your pocket. You a big man, Floyd. People supposed to treat you like a big man. You go down there and tell Jack Smitty that you ain't playing no Mother's Day dance unless he give you a piece of the pie... on top of your fee. And you tell Mr. T.L. Hall you tired of him turning your big money into little money. Tell him to turn your little money into big money and you'll give him the little piece. If he can't take the little piece tell him don't take nothing. You can't go up to Chicago and be a poor man. A poor man have it rough. I might have to cut me somebody the first day. Vera don't want that.

FLOYD. How you know what Vera want?

CANEWELL. I know Vera longer than you have. I know what kind of woman she is. Vera a quiet woman. Chicago's a noisy city. Anybody can tell you the two don't fit together.

FLOYD. Chicago is what you make it. It got some quiet parts. It got whatever you want. That's why everybody go there. That's why I'm going there. I'm going there to take advantage

of the opportunity. I'm gonna put out some more records. I
know what will make a hit record. I leave here on the
Greyhound and I bet you in one years time I be back driving a
Buick. Might even have a Cadillac. If you come visit me you
be able to use my telephone. I'm gonna have everything. Some
nice furniture. The white man ain't the only one can have a car
and nice furniture. Nice clothes. It take a fool to sit around
and don't want nothing. I ain't no fool. It's out there for
somebody it may as well be out there for me. If Vera go up
there with me and she don't like it I'll send her back. But at
least she will have the chance to see the opportunities.

(RED CARTER enters. He has been walking fast.)

RED CARTER. Hey, Floyd.

FLOYD. Hey, Red. *(To CANEWELL.)* Once she see the
opportunities she can make up her mind. But I'm gonna make
sure she see them.

RED CARTER. I'm on my way back down to my cousins's
house. He bought some of that insurance. He's pretty upset
about it. There's a whole bunch of people who bought some.
They got it in the paper. They say he sold over fifty thousand
dollars worth.

FLOYD. Fifty thousand dollars worth of what? What insurance? They got what in the paper?

RED CARTER. They got it in there about Mr. T.L. Hall.
(He gradually realizes they don't know.) Mr. T.L. Hall got arrested for selling fake insurance. Say he sold over fifty thousand dollars worth. Him and a fellow named Robert Gordon
was selling fake insurance for the Security Mutual something
or another.

CANEWELL. No wonder you couldn't find him. Who told you that, Red.

RED CARTER. My cousin bought some. The police was talking to him about it. They got it in the paper. Had his picture and everything. I thought you all knew.

FLOYD. *(Quietly.)* I had seven ways to go. They cut that down to six. I say let me try one of them six. They cut it down to five. Everytime I push... they pull. They cut it down to four. I say what's the matter? Everything can't go wrong all the time. They cut it down to three. I say three is better than two I really don't need but one. They cut it down to two. See... I'm going to Chicago. If I have to buy me a graveyard and kill everybody I see. I am going to Chicago. I don't want to live my life without. Everybody I know live without. I don't want to do that. I want to live with. I don't know what you all think of yourself but I think I'm supposed to have. Whatever it is. Have something. Have anything. My mama lived and died she ain't had nothing. If it ain't nothing but peace of mind then let me have that. My mama ain't had two dimes to rub together. And ain't had but one stick. She got to do without the fire. Some kind of warmth in her life. I don't want to live in a cold house. It's a cold world let me have a little shelter from it. That's all I want. Floyd Barton is gonna make his record. Floyd Barton is going to Chicago.

(FLOYD exits the yard.)

CANEWELL. Floyd! Floyd!

(CANEWELL goes to catch. FLOYD. The lights go down on the scene.)

Scene 4

(The lights come up on the yard. RED CARTER sits with VERA and LOUISE and RUBY. VERA is making her crêpe paper flowers.)

RED CARTER. That used to be enough. Get you five pounds of cornmeal, a couple of eggs and some milk—even if it wasn't nothing but powdered milk—and make you a meal. Put that with some beans and rice and what more is there? That used to be enough. It used to be alright to have you a rooster. Once upon a time in America it used to be alright to have a rooster in your yard. Now that done changed. It used to be you could leave your door open. Now you got to bar the roof. Ain't nothing went right since I broke that mirror. That ain't but three years ago. That's what scares me. I got four more years of bad luck. I was down Seefus... lost all my money. I was going good too. At one time I had forty dollars. I started to get up and leave but then I was trying to get forty more. Seem like everything broke down. Look over there. You got... One. Two. Three. Look there. You got seven birds sitting on that fence. You can count them. They sitting all in a row. If that dog next door start to howling I know something. It sure hurt me to pawn my pistol. I don't feel right without it. There's too many people out there act crazy. Too many people with knives. Icepicks. Meat cleavers and everything else. They had one fellow got in a fight with somebody and pulled a hatchet out from under his coat.

VERA. *(She crosses up to the gate.)* They called the dog-catcher on Miss Tillery's dog. Say she got to get a license.

LOUISE. He ought to have a license. That's how you know he belong to somebody.

RUBY. All you got to do is watch him and see where he go when he go home. You don't need no license for that.

RED CARTER. You need a license for everything. You need a license to fish in the river. The dog need a license. You need a license to sing on the street. You need a license to sell peanuts. Soon, you mark my words, soon you need license to walk down the street.

VERA. Hey Red what did Floyd say again?

RED CARTER. He say he was going to Chicago to make his record and wasn't nothing gonna stop him. Then he took off. We tried to go with him but he wouldn't let us. I don't know what's taking Canewell so long. He was supposed to go on the North side while I looked down around by the 88. Then we was supposed to meet here.

LOUISE. Vera you look sleepy.

VERA. I didn't go to bed till quarter to four. I was waiting on Floyd. Time I lay down everything was quiet and still. It stayed that way a long time. Then it started to move a little bit. You could hear the birds flying. They make a noise when they flap they wings. Then they started to sing. I started to get mad till I noticed it was daylight. The whole night passed and I didn't even know it. Floyd never did come.

RED CARTER. Canewell might've found him. I went and looked all the places I was supposed to. I looked down the 88. I looked down Taylor's. I looked down the House of Blues. Joe Burton's Pool Room. I looked all over. I even went up on Herron Avenue by the car barn.

(CANEWELL enters.)

CANEWELL. I couldn't find him.

VERA. Did you look down Irv's?

CANEWELL. I been all over. I been everywhere. Irv's. Hartzberger's. The Loendi Club. The Aurora Club. The Workingmen's Club. I don't know where he could be. You seen him, Red?

RED CARTER. Naw, I looked all the places we said. I couldn't find him.

LOUISE. I can't for the life of me place no Mr. T.L. Hall.

CANEWELL. You don't remember him? Used to go around selling insurance. That's how Floyd met him. Had a black Ford. A black shiny Ford.

RED CARTER. Used to wear a straw hat all the time. I believe he wore a straw hat even in the Winter.

LOUISE. I know who you talking about now. Had that old nasty looking hat. Used to wear it pushed back on his head.

VERA. That's him!

LOUISE. I never would have guessed that he was selling fake insurance.

CANEWELL. That's what the whole idea was... he didn't want you to guess it. If you could have guessed then he couldn't have sold nobody no insurance.

LOUISE. It's a shame the way they do the poor people.

CANEWELL. There's lots of poor people. Mr. T.L. Hall say he didn't want to be one. Selling that fake insurance might have been his only chance not to be poor... *(There is a sudden and loud commotion coming from MISS TILLERY'S yard. A dog barks. A woman wails. A rooster crows. There is a whole cacophony of barnyard sounds.)* Something done happened.

Something got them upset. They don't make noise like that unless they get agitated about something. I'm gonna go see what happened.

RED CARTER. I'll go with you.

(CANEWELL and RED CARTER exit the yard. VERA tries to look over the fence.)

LOUISE. What you see, Vera. What's going on?

VERA. Miss Tillery's kneeling down on the ground. I can't tell what's going on. She just sitting there. There some other people over there.

(HEDLEY enters the yard singing. He is wearing his business coat. He has his apron wrapped around something.)

HEDLEY. *(Singing.)*
"It's my pussin
It's my pussin
Take off your hand from she
Don't touch my pussin at all
It's my pussin
It's my pussin
I say you got no argument
for the pussin belong to me
It's my pussin..."

HEDLEY. *(cont.)* Hey. Womens. It's a good day. Fact of the matter is it's a great day. I go see the black boss man. I go see Joe Roberts you know. "The one hand wash the other," you know that saying?

LOUISE. Last time I seen you like this you had a pocketful of money.

HEDLEY. You are a smart woman. I always like you because you are a smart woman. Come let's dance. *(He dances around the yard.)* You don't want to dance. Okay. I am soon going to be a big man.

VERA. What you got there?

HEDLEY. Where? Oh this? When I was a little boy I learn about Toussaint L'Ouverture in the school. Miss Manning. She say listen you little black-as-sin niggers, you never each and none of you amount to nothing, you grow up to cut the white man cane and your whole life you never can be nothing as God is my witness, but I will tell you of a black boy who was a man and made the white man run from the blood in the street. Like that you know. Then she tell us about Toussaint L'Ouverture. I say I going to be just like that. Everybody say that you know. I go home and my daddy he sitting there and he big and black and tired taking care of the white man's horses and I say how come you not like Toussaint L'Ouverture why you do nothing? And he kick me with him boot in my mouth. I shut up that day you know and then when Marcus Garvey come he give me back my voice to speak. It was on my father's death bed, with Death standing there I say to him, "Father, I sorry about Toussaint L'Ouverture, Miss Manning say nobody ever amount to nothing and I never did again try. Then Marcus Garvey come and say that it was not true and that she lied and I forgive you kick me and I hope as God is with us now but a short time more that you forgive me my tongue." It was hard to say these things but I confess my love for my father and Death standing there say, "I already took him a half hour ago." And he cold as a boot, cold as a stone and hard like iron. I cried a river of tears but he was too heavy to float on them. So I dragged him with me these years across an ocean. Then my father come to me in a dream and say he was sorry he died without forgiving me my tongue and that he would send Buddy Bolden with some money for me to buy a plantation. Then I get the letter from the white man who come to take me away. So I say, Hedley, be smart, go and see Joe Roberts. We sat and talked man to man. Joe Roberts is a nice man. I told him about Toussaint L'Ouverture and my father and Joe Roberts smile and he say he had something to give me. And he give to me this. *(He takes out a machete that is wrapped in his burlap apron.)* Now Hedley ready for the white man when he come to take him away.

(The lights go down on the scene.)

Scene 5

(Lights come up on the yard. It is late at night. The neighborhood is asleep. HEDLEY is on guard with the machete in his hand. He struggles to stay awake by rocking back and forth chanting and singing.)

HEDLEY. Ain't no grave... can hold my body down
Ain't no grave... can hold my body down
Ain't no grave... can hold my body down. *(He begins to walk around the yard in a circle. Dogs are heard barking intermittently throughout the scene.)* You think the black man a dog in the dust you can kick when you want? I am not a dog!

You think you can throw a bone and I run after it. You think I
fetch for you and wag my tail for you. The black man is not a
dog! He is the lion of Judah! He is the mud God make his
image from. Ethiopia shall stretch forth her wings! The black
man is not a dog! I will stir up the dust around me like the
eagle stirreth its nest. Like a hurricane I will come through the
house. I will make the roof fall! I will stir up the dust around
me to let you know I talk this... *(He shoves the machete up
into the air.)* Ain't no grave can hold my body down. The black
man is not a dog. You think I come when you call. I wag my
tail. Look, I stirreth the nest. I am a hurricane to you when you
look at me you will see the house falling on your head. Its
roof and its shutters and all the windows broken.

(RUBY enters from the stairs.)

RUBY. Hedley what you doing? What you making all that
noise for?

(HEDLEY sees RUBY.)

HEDLEY. You think the black man is a dog that I will crawl
to you. I am a man, woman. I am the man to father your children. I offer you a kingdom! What you say I am a blind man?
I cast my pearls before swine?
RUBY. Hush all the noise. Be quiet! What's wrong with
you?

(RUBY starts toward HEDLEY.)

HEDLEY. I am not a blind man! I will not crawl for you. I

am a warrior. When I am in this dust my knees buckle from war not, from a woman! I offer you a kingdom. The flesh of my flesh, my seven generations... and you laugh at me! You laugh at Joe Louis's father! I offer you to be the Lily of the Valley. To be Queen of Sheba. Queen of the black man's Kingdom. You think I am a clown. I am the Lion of Judah!

RUBY. Hedley stop all that.

HEDLEY. Satan! I will tear your kingdom down!
Satan! I will tear your kingdom down!
Satan! I will tear your kingdom down!

(RUBY goes to HEDLEY and takes the machete from him. She lays it down on the bench. HEDLEY grabs her and kisses her violently. He is feverish with lust. He tries to find an opening to touch flesh.)

RUBY. Slow down, baby. It's alright. Ruby help you. Here. Ruby help you.

(RUBY lifts her dress and gives herself to HEDLEY out of recognition of his great need. The lights go down on the scene.)

Scene 6

(The lights come up on the yard. It is early evening. FLOYD is burying something in the garden. He smooths out the dirt with his feet. He has a guitar case and a dress box with him. He calls for VERA to come to the window.)

FLOYD. Hey... Vera!... Vera!

(VERA comes to the window. FLOYD holds the guitar up triumphantly.)

VERA. *(From window.)* Floyd where you been? You been gone for two days. Ain't nobody seen you.

(VERA enters. Floyd picks up the guitar to show her.)

FLOYD. Look at this! Look at this! That's the same kind of guitar as Muddy Waters got. Same color and everything...

VERA. Floyd that's brand new.

FLOYD. Wait till you hear how it sound. We ain't gonna talk about how nice it look till after you hear how it sound. To do that you got to come to the Blue Goose... The number One Blues Club in Pittsburgh... where the one and only Floyd "Schoolboy" Barton is appearing this Sunday... One night only... Mother's Day... Courtesy of Savoy Records. Come one come all to hear him perform his hit record "That's All Right" along with his new songs and future hits. That ain't all. Wait till you see this here. *(He takes a dress from the box.)* Size nine. That's your size.

VERA. Floyd it's beautiful. I don't believe it. I ain't never had nothing like this.

FLOYD. If you gonna be with Floyd Barton you got to go down to the Blue Goose looking nice.

VERA. Floyd where you been? Where you get all this from?

FLOYD. You know better than to ask me where I get anything from. I took a chance. Lots of times in life you taking a chance. Some people say that's all life is. Say I'm gonna take a chance on this... and I'm gonna take a chance on that... and I'm gonna take a chance on the other. And then sometimes you be taking your last chance. If you taking your last chance then you done used up your life. I say I'm just getting started and I didn't want to take no chance of not getting back up to Chicago. So yeah, I took a chance. I went out there to pay the gravestone man the rest of the money. He had the gravestone already made up. It's grey marble. It say Maude Avery Barton. Got two roses. One on each side. It looked so pretty. He say he have it on the grave by Mother's Day. We gonna go out there and see it. I left out of there and went down to the Greyhound bus station. Look here... *(He pulls some tickets from his pocket.)* What that say? Pittsburgh to Chicago. I told the man to write your name on it... he said they didn't do that. I took a pencil and wrote in on there myself. *(He shows VERA the ticket.)* Then I made a long distance phone call... cost me three dollars and ten cents. I called Mr. Wilber H. Gardner President of Savoy Records and told him I would be there on the 10th of June. Then I called the Delaware Towers Hotel on State Street and told them to get ready their best room for Miss Vera Dotsun... soon to be Mrs. Floyd Barton. That is... if she say Yeah.

VERA. I want to say yeah, but what am I saying yeah to? Another heartache? Another time for you to walk out the door with another woman?

FLOYD. You was there too, Vera. You had a hand in whatever it was. Maybe all the times we don't know the effect of what we do. But we cause what happens to us. Sometimes even in little ways we can't see. I went up to Chicago with Pearl Brown cause she was willing to believe that I could take her someplace she wanted to go. That I could give her things that she wanted to have. She told me by that... it was possible.

Even sometimes when you question yourself... when you wonder can you really make the music work for you... can you find a way to get it out into the world so it can burst in the air and have it mean something to somebody. She didn't know if I could do that. If I could have a hit record. But she was willing to believe it. Maybe it was selfish of her. Maybe she believed for all the wrong reasons. But that gave me a chance to try. So yeah... I took it. It wasn't easy. I was scared. But when them red lights came on in that recording studio it was like a bell ringing in the boxing match and I did it! I reached down inside me and I pulled out whatever was there. I did like my mama told me. I did my best. And I figured nobody could fault me for that. Then when they didn't release the record, Pearl Brown left. She thought she had believed wrong. I don't fault her for that. But I never lost the belief in myself. Then when they released the record I realized I didn't have nothing but a hit record. I come back to you figuring you couldn't say no to a man who got a hit record. But you did. And that made me see that you wanted more than Pearl Brown. I'm here saying I can give it to you. Try me one more time and I'll never jump back on you in life.

VERA. I got to thinking and I went down to the Greyhound Bus Station too. *(She hands him a ticket.)* Here. See that? What that say? It say one way... Chicago to Pittsburgh. It's good for one year from date of purchase. I'm gonna put that in my shoe. When we get to Chicago I'm gonna walk around on it. I hope I never have to use it.

FLOYD. Well, that's alright.

(The lights go down on the scene.)

Scene 7

(The lights come up on the yard. LOUISE is dressed for the Blue Goose. She calls up to the window for VERA. When she doesn't get a response, she goes to sit on the bench and wait. She talks to herself.)

LOUISE. I know it don't take all day to get dressed. I'm dressed. Seem like everybody should be dressed. My mother used to tell me I was gonna be late for my own funeral. She might be right. But then I won't have to worry about getting a seat. I don't know if I can take it no more. They about to drive me crazy. The House of Blues, the Blue Goose, the Red Carter, the dead rooster, the this-that-and-the-other, hurry up and sit down and let's dance and give me a drink and what I got? Who ain't don't know where the other one is or went or ain't going or is going and this one's dead and that one's dying and who shot who and who sung what song and give me another drink and her go a dollar and I ain't got a dime and what's the use and who to do and where ain't you been cause being all ain't no telling. *(VERA enters.)* And don't you know her and Hedley went to church. I liked to fell out. She say. "Aunt Louise I'm going to church with Hedley." That child ain't set foot in a Church since she was six years old on a Easter Sunday past the time ten years after I had quit going! Then on Thursday they going to the sanitarium. She talked him into going. You know Hedley wouldn't listen to nobody. I tried to talk him into going. You tried to talk him into going. Ain't no telling who else tried to talk him into going. He sit out here with a butcher knife. Sit out here with a machete ranting and raving and carrying on. She come along and he's gonna up an run to the sanitarium. Act like he anxious to get there. I don't understand it.

VERA. Ruby seem like she got a way about her that the men take to.

LOUISE. I wouldn't be surprised if there wasn't something between them. I done seen stranger things. He told me himself. Say he was gonna go down there and get tested. I just looked at him. I asked myself... *(RUBY enters.)* Where's Hedley?

RUBY. He's not here.

LOUISE. I thought you went to church with him.

RUBY. I did. After we got out of church he said he wanted to go see his friend. I stopped by the drugstore and I thought he be here by now.

LOUISE. Who? What friend?

RUBY. I don't know. Just some friend.

LOUISE. He didn't tell you who it was?

RUBY. I didn't ask him. He just said he was gonna go see... Bridge I think his name was.

LOUISE. Jim Breckenridge?

RUBY. Yeah. That sounds like it.

LOUISE. He gone down there to get some of that nasty moonshine. You ought to have brought him back here with you. Man go from church to the moonshine house. Talking about Ethiopia shall spread for the her wings and he won't be able to walk up the street.

VERA. He'll be back soon, Louise. Don't worry about him.

RUBY. I talked to him. He said he was gonna go down and get tested.

LOUISE. It ain't gonna do him no good. Not the way he been around here spitting up blood.

RUBY. I hope he live long enough to see this baby born.

LOUISE. Say what?

RUBY. I'm gonna tell him it's his. He's the only man who ever wanted to give me something. And I want to have that. He wants to be the father of my child. And that's what this child needs. I don't know about this messiah stuff but if it's a boy—and I hope God it is—I'm gonna name it after him. I'm gonna name him King

(CANEWELL enters. He has a newspaper under his arm.)

CANEWELL. Who's this? Wait a minute. Wait a minute. Let me see if I got my knife. I go down to the Blue Goose with you all and I know I'm gonna have to cut three or four people. Good as you all look. Louise, you look like Queen Ester and Vera look like the Queen of Sheba.

LOUISE. Go on with that stuff man.

CANEWELL. What's the matter Ruby ain't you going?

RUBY. *(Ignoring him.)* I got to go get ready.

(RUBY exits upstairs.)

VERA. What the paper say about Ms. Tillery's boy?

CANEWELL. "Policeman Foils Robbery." The policeman was standing there getting his shoes shined. He was loafing on the job and ended up being a hero. They mayor liable to give him a medal. *(Reads.)* "A robbery at the loan offices of Metro Finance ended in the death of a Hill District man Friday. Williard Ray Tillery, 27, an unemployed laborer was shot and killed while fleeing the scene of the crime. Police say the suspect fired two shots at Officer Haywood who returned the fire striking the suspect in the back." How come the police is the only one who always shoot straight. Everybody else miss. They may as well not even bother to shoot.

VERA. I didn't know Poochie was that young. I thought he was older.

LOUISE. They come and told her Poochie and she commenced to moaning. The bible say mourn for three days... she started her three days right there. She was out there for about eight hours crying. "My Poochie boy. My Poochie boy." She didn't go into the house till the next morning. They had to get her sister to come from Wheeling, West Virginia. She finally talked her into going in. She just kept saying, "My Poochie boy. My Poochie boy."

CANEWELL. *(Reads.)* "Police are searching for two other men believed to be accomplices who police say escaped with an undisclosed amount of cash." See that's another thing. I know how the police do. They shoot the man in the back. Take the money out his hand and put it in their pocket and say, "Oh, the other ones got away with the money. We still looking for them."

LOUISE. That's a shame any mother have to go through that.

CANEWELL. All Poochie wanted was to be a bricklayer.

LOUISE. He laying bricks in hell now.

CANEWELL. He might have went to heaven now. You don't know. The devil don't take everybody you think he ought to. *(He calls.)* Floyd! Comeon man!

LOUISE. Let me go up there and see how this child's getting on. Don't you all leave without me.

(LOUISE exits upstairs. VERA and CANEWELL sit in awkward silence.)

VERA. Canewell, Floyd and me are gonna get married. See if we can make it.

CANEWELL. I always did believe in love. I felt like if you don't believe in love you may as well not believe in nothing. Even love that ain't but halfway is still love. And that don't make it no less cause its only coming one way. If it was two ways it still be the same amount of love. Just like say I loved you and you didn't love me back. I can still say I'm all filled up with love for Vera. I go walking down the street people can see that. They don't know what to call it but they can see something going on. Maybe they see a man who look like he satisfied with life and that make him walk more better. Make him walk like he got a million dollars in his pocket. If I loved you and this time you loved me back. I don't see where my love for you can get more bigger that it already was. Unless I walk like I got two million dollars. Sometime people don't count it if you ain't loved back. But I count it all the same. Some women make their bed up so high don't nobody know how to get to it. I know you ain't like that. You know how to make your bed up high and turn you lamp down low. That's why Floyd don't want to lose you. I think you and Floyd ought to go ahead and see what you all can make of it.

(LOUISE enters.)

LOUISE. Bella need to fix these steps. She been saying that for the longest time.

(The sound of a rooster crowing is heard from Miss Tillery's.)

VERA. Miss Tillery got her another rooster.

LOUISE. She ought to have gone to Woolworths and got her an alarm clock.

CANEWELL. *(Calls.)* Hey Floyd!... Comeon! The people is waiting! (RED CARTER enters through the gate.) I called Floyd. I ain't called you. I thought you was setting up the drums.

RED CARTER. That don't take all day. I come by here to see what was keeping you all. The people is starting to come. Where's Floyd?

CANEWELL. He getting ready.

LOUISE. How you doing, Red?

RED CARTER. Who is that calling my name?

LOUISE. Oh, hush up, man. You ought to be able to tell me in the dark.

RED CARTER. I didn't say I couldn't.

VERA. Here, Red I got you a flower for Mother's Day. What color you need?

RED CARTER. I need a red flower. My mother still living and even as I know it got to come to the day I wear a white flower... I hope it ain't no time soon.

(VERA pins the flower on RED CARTER. FLOYD enters from the house. He is dressed for performing and carries an electric guitar.)

LOUISE. Ohhhh. You look sharp. Look at him Vera.

VERA. Don't he look good. I told him I like that suit.

FLOYD. This some Chicago style. I bought this suit in Chicago. Canewell was there with me. I was telling Vera, they got some nice clothes for women up there too.

RED CARTER. They waiting on you down there. I got my drums set up and they got J.D. Lawrence warming up the house.

FLOYD. I ain't in no hurry. Let them wait. They can't do nothing without me. —You got your harmonica?

(CANEWELL takes out his harmonica and blows.)

CANEWELL. The train leaving the station.

FLOYD. Well alright.

RED CARTER. Where Ruby?

FLOYD. I got to get on now. If she going she better come on.

CANEWELL. *(Calls.)* Hey, Ruby!

(RUBY comes down the stairs. She is wearing a red dress.)

RUBY. Is these stockings straight?

(FLOYD and CANEWELL look at her and stop dead in their tracks. The lights go down to black.)

Scene 8

(The lights come up on the yard. FLOYD, VERA, LOUISE and CANEWELL enter. They have come back from the Blue Goose.)

CANEWELL. I didn't know there was gonna be that many

people. People was crowded in everywhere. They was crowded all the way up in the back, into the corners. J.C. had to close the door, and still had people outside trying to get in.

LOUISE. I thought the floor was gonna cave in with all them people. Then Floyd got up on that stage and started playing that guitar... the people started to hollering and carrying on and then I thought the roof was gonna cave in. And Canewell... I thought that harmonica was going out of style! The way you was blowing on that thing. *(She sings.)*

"That's ALL Right
I know you're in love with another man
But That's ALL Right..."

LOUISE. *(cont.)* I see you all tomorrow. Hedley's probably up there asleep. I can't wait to see Red Carter. He got down there and act like he didn't even know me. Wait till I get him straight. I see you all tomorrow. Good night.

VERA. Good night.

FLOYD. I see you tomorrow, Louise.

CANEWELL. Watch your step now. *(LOUISE exits. CANEWELL notices the roots of the Golden Seal plant are uncovered.)* Whoa! What happened here? Vera, the roots on this plant gonna dry out and rot. You supposed to put them in the ground. This plant gonna die.

VERA. Hedley planted it. I don't know how it got like that.

CANEWELL. I'll fix it for you. Where Hedley keep them shovels?

VERA.. Somewhere over there.

(CANEWELL goes over to HEDLEY'S area.)

FLOYD. We'll fix it. You go in the house and get ready.

When I was up there singing "Good Rocking Tonight" what you think I was talking about?

VERA. I hope I ain't got it wrong. I'll be waiting for you. I like that other song too. What you call it "Sixty Minute Man."

(CANEWELL has found the shovel and begins to dig in the garden as VERA exits. FLOYD turns around just as CANEWELL unearths a blue handkerchief with $1200 in tens and twenties. He stoops to pick it up.)

CANEWELL. What is this?
FLOYD. That's mine!

(FLOYD tries to snatch it out of CANEWELL'S hand.)

CANEWELL. Look at this! Look at this! This must be Hedley's stash. Everybody says he don't trust no banks. Scared the white man gonna cheat him.

FLOYD. Give it to me. It's mine.

CANEWELL. How this gonna be yours when I found it.

FLOYD. Cause I said it is. You ain't got to know nothing else. I said its mine you supposed to give it to me.

CANEWELL. Naw, naw. Finder's Keepers. Didn't you learn that in kindergarten?

(FLOYD tries to wrestle the money away form CANEWELL.)

FLOYD. Give me my money!

CANEWELL. You can't just take it from me! How you just gonna take it from me!

FLOYD. I said it's mine.

CANEWELL. I don't care what you said. You can't just take it from me. I ain't gonna let nobody take nothing from me.

(FLOYD pulls his gun on CANEWELL.)

FLOYD. Give me my money!

(CANEWELL stares at FLOYD in disbelief.)

CANEWELL. Hey, Floyd... this is me... Canewell.
FLOYD. I don't care who you are. Give me my money!
CANEWELL. How this gonna be yours when...

(FLOYD cocks back the hammer.)

FLOYD. Give me my money!

(CANEWELL suddenly realizes the truth.)

CANEWELL. You and Poochie.
FLOYD. Give me my money!
CANEWELL. Here, Floyd. You got it. Here.
FLOYD. Poochie took a chance. We both took a chance.
CANEWELL. I understand, Floyd. I understand.

(CANEWELL hands FLOYD the money and exits. FLOYD counts off some money, puts it in his pocket. He stands exposed in a shaft of the light counting the rest of the money when HEDLEY enters. HEDLEY sees FLOYD in the yard. He stops and rubs his eyes. He begins to laugh. It is an odd mixture of laughter and tears. He has waited many years

for this moment.)

HEDLEY. Buddy... you come. You come Buddy. Oh, how I wait for you. So long I wait for you. I think to myself many times "Maybe I die before Buddy Bolden bring me my father's money." Maybe I'm not going to be a big man after all. Maybe my father don't forgive me, but I see you have the money. Give it to me.

FLOYD. Get out of here, Hedley. You been drinking that rot gut. Go on in the house.

HEDLEY. But I see I was wrong. I see you have the money. Give me the money, Buddy.

FLOYD. I ain't playing no game now. Go on in the house and go to bed.

HEDLEY. No Buddy, give me the money. You say, "Come here... here go the money." Give it to me. It's my father's money. Give it to me.

FLOYD. Comeon now! Watch it! Go on in the house. *(HEDLEY attempts to take the money from FLOYD. FLOYD pushes him down to the ground.)* I told you to go on now! *(FLOYD helps HEDLEY get up.)* Here. Comeon. Go on in the house now. I'll see you tomorrow.

(HEDLEY gets up and exits into the cellar as FLOYD begins to bury the money again. HEDLEY comes from the cellar carrying the machete. FLOYD, hearing him approach, turns and HEDLEY severs his windpipe with one blow.)

HEDLEY. This time Buddy... you give me the money.

(The lights go down on the scene.)

Scene 9

(The lights come up on the yard. "That's All Right" plays on the victrola from VERA'S apartment. LOUISE, CANEWELL, RED CARTER, and HEDLEY are in the yard.)

RED CARTER. Floyd "Schoolboy" Barton.

LOUISE. Hedley up here going to sleep.

HEDLEY. I'm not sleep, woman.

CANEWELL. Hedley say he resting When you see him sitting down he thinking about what he gonna do when he get up.

RED CARTER. What the police say, Louise?

LOUISE. They ain't said nothing. They was out here again looking around in the yard this morning. Asking everybody questions.

CANEWELL. They come by my house too. Asking all kinds of questions. At first they was trying to act like I done it. I was glad they got that idea out their head.

LOUISE. They don't know who done it. They still trying to figure it out.

(RUBY enters from the stairs carrying a blanket.)

RUBY. Somebody need to put a light in that bathroom. The bulb done burnt out. I want a beer.

RED CARTER. That's what I told Vera. It don't cost but two dollars and fifty cents a case.

(VERA enters from her apartment.)

RUBY. Take me down the street and buy me a beer.

RED CARTER. I'll buy you two beers. And anything else you want. Comeon.

VERA. You leaving, Red?

RED CARTER. Yeah, I'm gonna go. I'm gonna take Ruby and buy her a beer.

RUBY. *(To HEDLEY.)* Here put this on. I'm going down the street with Red. I'll be back.

RED CARTER. Canewell, I'll see you down the House of Blues sometime.

CANEWELL. Not if I see you first.

LOUISE. Hey, Red... comeon back and I'll play you some two hand pinochle.

RED CARTER. I can't play no pinochle.

LOUISE. That's all right I'll teach you.

RED CARTER. Well alright. I'll see you Vera.

(RED CARTER and RUBY exit.)

LOUISE. Comeon Vera, I'll help you with the dishes.

(LOUISE starts into the house.)

VERA. I started walking away from there feeling bad. I turned to look back and Floyd was floating up above the ground. Them six men was holding him up. He come right out the casket just like they laid him in there and was floating up in the air. I could see where they was carrying him. They was all floating up in the sky. I tried to call Floyd's name but wouldn't nothing come out my mouth. Seem like he started to move faster. I say the only thing. I can do here is say good-bye. I waved at him and he went on up in the sky.

(VERA and LOUISE exit. CANEWELL and HEDLEY sit and stare at each other. The silence swells.)

CANEWELL. *(Singing.)* "I thought I heard
Buddy Bolden say..."
HEDLEY. What he say?
CANEWELL. He say, "Wake up and give me the money."
HEDLEY. Naw. Naw. He say, "Come here, here go the money."
CANEWELL. What he give you?
HEDLEY. He give me this.

(HEDLEY hold up a handful of crumpled bills. The slip from his fingers and fall to the ground like ashes.)

HEDLEY. *(Singing.)* "I thought I heard
Buddy Bolden say...
I thought I heard
Buddy Bolden say...
I thought I heard
Buddy Bolden say..."

(The lights go down to BLACK.)

END OF PLAY

PROP INVENTORY

Furniture:
    Bench
    Card table
    Table crate
    Yellow chair
    2 - Red chairs
    Green chair
    Small wooden crate
    Hedley stool

Props:
    3 - chicken crates
    3 - fake chickens
    4 - live Rhode Island Red chickens (or fake facsimiles)
    Rooster rigged with blood
    Reel blood
    Hedley crate
    Hedley counter
    2 - buckets
    Funnel
    Coal bucket w/coal
    Kerosene jug with water
    Bag of feathers
    1-string
    1-string crate
    1-string rock
    Hammer
    Coke bottle
    Machete wrapped in apron

Baby Ruth box filled with weight
Empty Baby Ruth box
2 - butterfinger boxes
2 - Clark boxes
5 - Chesterfield cartons taped together
3 - Chesterfield cartons (one is practical)
Water hose
Leather Apron
Hedley towel
Brush
Cutting board
2 - butcher knives
4 - knives
Knife can
Notebooks with pencil
5 - wire baskets (2 thrown)
Basket filled with eggs, sandwiches
3 - wrapped sandwiches
4 - loose eggs
Pickable crocus
Tuna can ashtray with sand
Smoke pot with sand
Kitchen ashtray
Small 3rd Floor ashtray
Golden seal rigged w/pull line
Golden seal with dirt base
Watering can
Wire crates/wash basin grill set-up
2 - shovels
Bamboo pole
2 - Clumps of peppers (1 with S hook)

3 - Pairs of drumsticks
3 - Harmonicas
2 - Pocket knives
2 - .38 guns (practical)
4 - blank cartridges, 1/4 charge smokeless
Snub-nose .32
2 - Old Crow pint bottles
3 - Imperial pint bottles
Black flowered tray
Blue pie plate
3 - saucers (pink, yellow, blue)
Green dinner plate
Rock glass
Water glass
3 - clear shiskey glasses
Green coffee mug
Yellow coffee cup
Caramel food coloring
4 - Dinner forks
Pie scooper
Blue bowl
Pot with handle
Brown paper bag w/cardboard base
Blue flowered towel
52 Red playing cards
RCA Victor radio w/practical speaker
3 - Bus tickets
Mesh bag with dress
Acoustic guitar in case
Electric guitar in case
2 - Red paper flowers with pins

1 - White paper flower with pin
10 - strips of white crêpe
10 - strips of red crêpe
Roll of red crêpe
Roll of white crêpe
2 - rolls of green florist tape
Bunch of flowers
Kitchen light with 2 hooks (practical)
Blanket
2 - Stacks of money
10 - 1 dollar bills
Rolled paper cigars
Barbecue pot w/sauce
Basting mop brush
Box of wax paper
2 - strips of wax paper
3 - chicken quarters
4 - catfish fillets
2 - shakers
Tongs
Bottle of hot sauce
10 - slices of edible white bread
17 -fresh collard greens
1/2 pint of cooked collard greens
1 - slice of sweet potatoe pie
2 - pieces of baked cornbread
Hardboiled brown egg
Box with tissue paper and dress
Red hanky
2 - letters from record co., unsealed
Letter from Elmore

Letter from board of health, no envelope
Postcard
Newspaper
Baby Wipes
Money changer
Suitcase, weighted
Durgstore bag with cocoa butter
Grocery bag
Fake bread
4 - fake vegetable stalks
2 - Zippo Lighters
Flints
Lighter fluid
8 - King Edwards Invin. DeLuxe cigars, wrapped
Cigar holder
6 - Diamond box matches
Strike Anywhere matches
2 - Chesterfield packs, filled with herbal cigs.
Old God pack, filled with herbal cigs.
2 - loose herbal cigarettes
Barbecue sauce

COSTUME INVENTORY

LOUISE:

    2 - piece black crêpe suit
    Green dress with black print
    Black, teal and yellow print dress
    White dress with blue polka dots
    Navy dress with white print
    Black slip
    Hosiery with seams
    Navy straw hat
    Black leather belt
    Navy fabric belt with white buckle
    Blue suede heels
    Blue wedgie shoes
    Red mule shoes
    Navy purse
    Red snakeskin purse
    White drop earrings
    Ivory rose brooch
    Pearl necklace
    White wrist gloves

RUBY:

    Yellow rayon dress
    Red and white rayon print dress
    Red backless dress
    Black crêpe dress
    Brown and blue jacket
    Full white slip
    Hosiery - seamed

Light brown straw hat
Black leather shoes
Black suede shoes with strap
Black purse with strap
Small blue faille change purse
Brown leather belt
Cream silk flower corsage
Red carnation hair ornament
Black silk flower corsage
Red hoop earrings
Yellow, orange, red bangle bracelets
Black drop earrings

VERA:

Black dress with rhinestones and peplum
Green leaf print dress
Burgundy starburst print dress
Green cotton plaid dress
Aqua or peach slip
Tan straw hat with pin
Hosiery - seamed
Black heels
White sling-back wedgie shoes
Small black clutch purse
Colorful floral hanky
Marcasite faux earrings

HEDLEY:

2 piece black suit
Light short-sleeved shirt
V-neck T-shirt

Black grey-striped pants
Beige wool jacket
Brown leather apron
White cotton apron
Black dress socks
Boot Socks
Black wing tip shoes
Black leather cap toe boots
Gray fedora hat
Black tie
Black leather suspenders
Wide black leather belt

CANEWELL:

Brown striped suit
Two-tone jacket
Red and white plaid shirt
Tan and Black striped shirt
Black and gold striped shirt
Grey/Cream plaid shirt
V-Neck T-Shirt
Black/grey wool pants
Dark brown and burgundy socks
Brown shoes
Light brown fedora hat
Burgundy belt
Brown, green and gold tie

FLOYD:

2 Piece dark blue pinstriped suit
Cream suit

Ochre shirt
Blue two-tone shirt
White shirt
Off-white sleeveless undershirt
Navy patterned socks
Beige socks
Orange leather and suede lace-up shoes
Two tone shoes
Gray fedora hat
Cream Panama hat
Belt
Gold pocket square
White silk pocket square
White silk tie
Gold tie chain

RED CARTER:
Brown striped suit
Beige plaid jacket
Purple shirt
Dark blue shirt
Red shirt
V-neck T-shirt
Dark brown shoes
Panama straw hat
Burgundy with blue suspenders
Burgundy pocket square
White pocket square
Gold pinkie ring

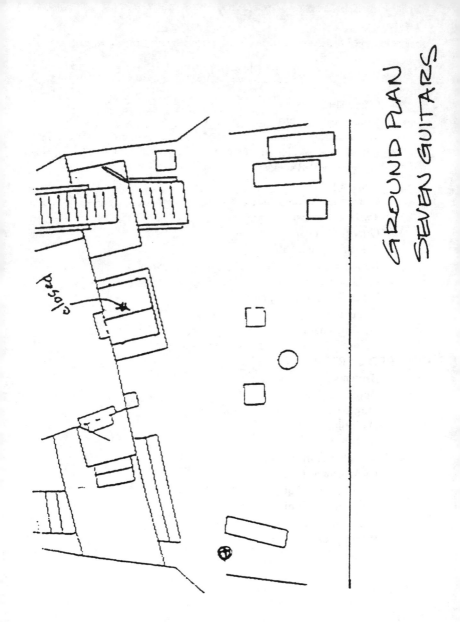

GROUND PLAN
SEVEN GUITARS

Other Publications For Your Interest

ROAD TO MECCA, THE. (Little Theatre.) Drama. Athol Fugard. 1m. 2f Int. 1988 Winner, "Best Foreign Play," New York Drama Critics Circle. This unusual play by one of the world's most important contemporary dramatists is *not* about the effects of apartheid in South Africa. In fact, there are no Black characters. The drama focuses on Miss Helen, an old Boer woman who lives alone out in the South African boondocks, where she creates an odd menagerie of concrete sculptures which she calls her "Mecca". Also in the play is Elsa Barlow, a young woman who was once helped by Miss Helen, and who has travelled hundreds of miles to her to help out in a time of crisis—Miss Helen, is in danger of being evicted and sent to an old-folks' home by a local narrow-minded minister named Marius, for whom Helen's sculptures are not art, but a public nuisance. A penetrating study of the role of the artist in any society, this important new play was produced both in London and in New York, to great critical acclaim. "The author's most personal play to date, an essential rosetta stone for the entire canon."—N.Y Times. "Glows with a rare luminosity and intensity. Athol Fugard's latest play . . . is also his most eloquent and transforming."—Ch. Sci. Mon. "One of Fugard's simplest, most beautiful plays."—N.Y Daily News **(#20101)**

MY CHILDREN! MY AFRICA! (Little Theatre.) Drama. Athol Fugard. 2m., 1f. Simple unit set. The great South African playwright once again confronts the terrible toll of apartheid in his native land in this compelling tale focusing on the efforts of a humble, humane, black school teacher in a segregated township to persuade just one young person that violence is not the answer to South Africa's problems, that the only hope is through education. Mr. M, the delightful teacher, is aided by a young white teenager named Isabel, who becomes friends with the black youth in the play, Thami, after besting him in a debate moderated by Mr. M. Thami is torn between his respect for Mr. M and his love for education and the anger and violence of his compatriots, which exerts a powerful pull on him. Eventually, he must choose which side he is on when the riots begin and his fellows accuse Mr. M of being an informer. He pleads with his teacher to announce that he has *not* named names to the police but of course, Mr. M *has* and, as a man who lives by the highest moral principles imparted from the world's great books, he stands by his decision to inform the police believing that, in the long run, violence only begets more violence, that ends do not justify means. In the end, Mr. M is beaten to death and set on fire by the angry mob, Thami goes off to join the revolution and Isabel alone remains to honor the memory of a gentle, Gandhian soul who actually had the temerity to believe that poetry was mightier than the sword. Only an Athol Fugard could, or would, dare to come up with such a cautionary tale (which is, by the way, inspired by a true incident), a warning against all violence, even that perpetrated in the name of a revolution against apartheid. "A document of towering stature."—Phila. Inquirer. "The drama vacillates superbly between political parable and personal tragedy."—Village Voice. **(#15218)**

Picasso at the Lapin Agile
STEVE MARTIN

"Very good fun."
NEW YORK TIMES
"Very funny ... [and] daring."
NEW YORK POST

This long-running Off-Broadway hit places Albert Einstein and Pablo Picasso in a Parisian cafe in 1904, just before the renowned scientist transformed physics and the celebrated painter set the world afire. In his first stage comedy, the popular actor and screenwriter plays fast and loose with fact, fame and fortune as these two geniuses interact with infectious dizziness. 7 m., 2 f. (#18962)

Arts & Leisure
STEVE TESICH

Written by the popular author of TOUCHING BOTTOM, ON THE OPEN ROAD, THE SPEED OF DARKNESS and other plays, this brilliantly caustic play is centered around a self-absorbed drama critic who judges theater and life by the same criteria, to absurd extremes. He is confronted by the bitter and alienated women who have suffered from his unyieldingly clinical detachment and his habit of judging their suffering by its dramatic effect on him. 1 m., 4 f. (#3866)

Samuel French, Inc.
SERVING THE THEATRICAL COMMUNITY SINCE 1830

DEATH DEFYING ACTS
David Mamet ● Elaine May ● Woody Allen

This Off-Broadway hit features comedies by three masters of the genre. David Mamet's brilliant twenty-minute play INTERVIEW is a mystifying interrogation of a sleazy lawyer. In HOTLINE, a wildly funny forty-minute piece by Elaine May, a woman caller on a suicide hotline overwhelms a novice counselor. A psychiatrist has discovered that her husband is unfaithful in Woody Allen's hilarious hour-long second act, CENTRAL PARK WEST. 2 m., 3 f. (#6201)

MOON OVER BUFFALO
Ken Ludwig

A theatre in Buffalo in 1953 is the setting for this hilarious backstage farce by the author of LEND ME A TENOR. Carol Burnett and Philip Bosco starred on Broadway as married thespians to whom fate gives one more shot at stardom during a madcap matinee performance of PRIVATE LIVES - or is it CYRANO DE BERGERAC? 4 m., 4 f. (#17)

Samuel French, Inc.
SERVING THE THEATRICAL COMMUNITY SINCE 1830

Racing Demon
DAVID HARE

"Riveting."
NEW YORK MAGAZINE
"David Hare ... can shake a soul."
TIME MAGAZINE

This award-winning play premiered at the Royal National Theatre and at Lincoln Center. Attracting unwanted publicity, the Church of England is racked with dissention over matters of doctrine and practice and is at odds with the government. Reverend Lionel Espy and his team of clery struggle within this volatile climate to make sense of their mission in South London. Winner of four prestigious "Best Play" awards. 8 m., 3 f. (#19956)

Sacrilege
DIANE SHAFFER

"A play charged with genuine ideas."
WCBS TELEVISION
"Compelling. SACRILEGE moved me to tears."
VARIETY

Ellen Burstyn starred on Broadway in this riveting drama about a devout Catholic nun who is fighting the Vatican to allow women in the priesthood. Her evenutal expulsion from her order forces others to re-examine the meaning of faith, spiritual violence and the redeeming grace of God. 6 m., 3 f. (#20977)

Samuel French, Inc.
SERVING THE THEATRICAL COMMUNITY SINCE 1830

The Radical Mystique
ARTHUR LAURENTS

"Achingly earnest comedy of manners."
THE NEW YORK TIMES
"Full of caustic wit and moments of wisdom."
NEW YORK DAILY NEWS

In the New York of the late 60's when "radical chic" was coined by Tom Wolfe, friends Josie and Janice are arranging a party to benefit the Black Panthers. In the process, their complacency is shaken and they are forced to confront realities they would rather ignore. 3 m., 5 f. (#19961)

Dog Opera
CONSTANCE CONGDON

"A singular work created by an imagination
of redeeming freedom and eccentricity."
THE NEW YORK TIMES

Peter and Madeline, who are now in their thirities, have been best friends since childhood. Even though they are more loving than most couples and both in search of a partner, they are fundamentally incompatible in this moving contemporary comedy that premiered at The Joseph Papp Public Theatre. 5 m., 2 f. (#3866)

Samuel French, Inc.
SERVING THE THEATRICAL COMMUNITY SINCE 1830

Other Publications for your Interest

PIANO LESSON, THE. (Black Groups). Drama.
by August Wilson.
5m., 3f Comb. Int.

Mr. Wilson won his second Pulitzer Prize for this haunting drama, part of a cycle of plays dealing with black life in these United States during separate decades. *The Piano Lesson* is set in 1936, in Pittsburgh. The central character, Boy Willie, has driven up from down home in the South with a battered truck full of watermelons to sell. He has an opportunity to buy some land down home; but he must come up with the money right quick or he'll lose out. Boy Willie, a human dynamo bursting with ideas and dreams, has a plan: He wants to sell a battered old piano which has been in his family for generations, which belongs half to him and half to his sister Berniece. The piano sits in Berniece's living room. She's had several offers for it, as it is not only an antique but is covered with incredible carvings detailing the family's rise up from slavery. She has turned them all down, though. For her the piano is a symbol of her family's past whereas for Boy Willie it is their hope for the future. Somehow, he must persuade his stubborn and defiant sister that the past is the past. Berniece turns out to be a more formidable foe than Boy Willie anticipated, though! "Joyously an African-American play: it has its own spacious poetry, its own sharp angle on a nation's history, its own metaphorical idea of drama and its own palpable ghosts . . . like other Wilson plays, it seems to sing even when it is talking."—N.Y. Times. "A lovely tragi-comedy. haunting as well as haunted."—N.Y. Newsday. "Wonderful . . . a play of magnificent confrontations."—N.Y. Post.

MA RAINEY'S BLACK BOTTOM. (Advanced Groups.) Play with music.
by August Wilson.
5 black m., 3 white m., 2 black f Unit set.

The time is 1927. The place is a rundown recording studio in Chicago. Ma Rainey, the legendary blues singer, is due to arrive with her Entourage to cut new sides of old favorites. Waiting for her are her Black musician sidemen, the White owner of the recording company. and her White manager. What goes down in the session to come is more than music. It is a riveting portrayal of Black rage . . . of racism, of the self-hate that racism breeds, and of racial exploitation. ". . . Wilson sends the history of Black America crashing down upon our heads . . . a searing inside account of what racism does to its victims . . . it is also funny, salty, carnal and lyrical . . . Wilson has lighted a dramatic fuse that snakes and hisses through several anguished eras of American life. When the fuse reaches its explosive final destination, the audience is impaled by the impact."—N.Y. Times. "What a joy! Brilliant . . . explosive! One of the most dramatically riveting plays I've seen in years."—Wm. Raidy, Newhouse Newspapers. Winner 1985, New York Drama Critics Circle Award.